Property of Veronica

P9-BYI-116

CHUTNEYS and RELISHES

LORRAINE BODGER

ILLUSTRATED BY LORRAINE BODGER

SIMON & SCHUSTER

NEW YORK   LONDON   TORONTO   SYDNEY   TOKYO   SINGAPORE

SIMON & SCHUSTER
Rockefeller Center
1230 Avenue of the Americas
New York, NY 10020

Designed by Bonni Leon-Berman

Manufactured in the United States of America
10 9 8 7 6 5 4 3 2 1
Library of Congress Cataloging-in-Publication Data
Bodger, Lorraine.
    Chutneys and relishes : more than 50 recipes for delicious, easy-to-prepare fruit and vegetable accompaniments / Lorraine Bodger ;
illustrated by Lorraine Bodger.
        p.   cm.
    Includes index.
    1. Chutney.   2. Cookery (Relishes)   I. Title.
TX819.A1B6   1995   95-32275
641.8'14—dc20   CIP
ISBN 0-684-81156-1

This book is dedicated to the memory of a farm in Phoenicia, New York, where so many things were done for the first time, not least of which was making chutneys and relishes.

CONTENTS

VEGETABLE CHUTNEYS AND RELISHES   83

Introduction

Anyone who has dined recently at a trendy American restaurant is no stranger to the tasty little mounds of spicy chutney or bright relish garnishing the plates these days. It's the chef's way of adding pizzazz to the simplest grilled chicken or fish or of adding a finishing touch to a more complex dish. And it makes the customer feel she's getting that extra something she wouldn't get at home.

True, there are many restaurant dishes you can't re-create at home, but chutneys and relishes aren't among them. On the contrary, these easy-to-prepare condiments are perfectly suited to home preparation, and they'll do the same thing for home-cooked meals that they do for restaurant ones: Add the finishing touch that turns a simple meal into a memorable one.

Take basic chicken, for example, season by season: In the fall, pair a whole roasted bird with Savory Apple-Onion Chutney or Spiced Pear Chutney with Pecans, and serve with baked sweet potatoes and a big green salad. In winter, a rich mixture such as Cranberry-Currant Relish with Port or Golden Carrot Chutney makes a company dinner out of baked chicken, wild rice and crisp broccoli. When spring comes, try cold poached chicken accompanied by Rhubarb-Raisin Chutney or Fennel Relish, French bread and either asparagus or sugar snap peas. And for summer, grill plenty of chicken quarters and fresh vegetables and serve with Summer Fruit Chutney and End-of-the-Garden Tomato Relish—a perfect outdoor meal.

Chutneys and relishes will give the same lift to turkey, duck, lamb, pork, veal and beef, not to mention baked or grilled fish, shrimp and other seafood. Vegetarians will love these condiments, too, since they go a long way toward improving steamed vegetables, baked potatoes, cooked grains, lentils and beans. Better yet, easy-to-make chutneys and relishes accomplish the miraculous: They add flavor and zip to meals without adding a lot of fat.

Chutneys (usually cooked) and relishes (usually uncooked) run the culinary gamut: They may be thick or thin, chunky or smooth, spicy or soothing, robustly or delicately seasoned. They may be tart, sweet, salty, pungent, piquant or any combination of these flavors. In winter they stimulate the taste buds; in summer they refresh them.

One fruit or vegetable usually predominates—as in peach chutney or cabbage relish—so you can work with whatever produce is most abundant in your garden or farmers' market, or choose whatever looks freshest in the grocery store. Spices, herbs and other seasonings are added, along with such ingredients as vinegar, sugar, grated lemon rind, ginger, garlic or hot pepper. The ingredients are so readily available that many cooks will have everything they need (except the main fruit or vegetable) in their pantries right now.

The secret of any good chutney or relish is the combination and proportion of ingredients, but the beauty of chutney or relish is the versatility, both in how you use it and how you make it. You're free to follow the recipes exactly for absolutely foolproof results or to take a little flyer according to your personal taste and what you have around the kitchen: If you don't have raisins, you can substitute currants or bits of dried apricot. If you have no peaches, make your chutney with nectarines instead. If you don't like balsamic vinegar, try cider vinegar instead. Too much garlic for your family? Use a little less.

As for cooking technique, you don't need much: Making chutneys and relishes is just a matter of a little chopping, a little sautéing, a little simmering—and sometimes not even that much. The recipes require no tedious canning and no more attentiveness or advanced cooking skills than it takes to make oatmeal. You will *not* be overwhelmed by cauldrons of simmering chutney; you will, in fact, make the perfect amount: enough for one or two meals, with a bit left over to slather on bread, stir into yogurt, or just nip from the bowl.

Which brings up the matter of exactly what your chutney or relish should be served with. The menu suggestions included with each recipe will give you some what-goes-with-what guidelines, but follow your taste buds as well. If I recommend lamb chops, but you're leaning toward broiled swordfish—by all means, try the fish.

Keep in mind, too, that chutneys and relishes are not just for dinner. Some chutneys and relishes make especially good appetizers when spooned onto crackers, toasted pita wedges or tortilla chips, while others are delicious as part of a smorgasbord or antipasto. A few will stand in as side dishes or salads. You can pack these treats in your picnic basket or have them at brunch or lunch, spread them on sandwiches or use them for dips. You can even put them on the table to perk up the take-out food you picked up on the way home from work.

Once you've tried a few of these recipes, with their simple ingredients, minimal work and delicious payoff, you'll never want to be without them.

Basics

Fresh, Fresh, Fresh

The chutneys and relishes made from these recipes are fresh and meant to be eaten as soon as possible—preferably immediately and certainly within a few days. Don't confuse these fresh condiments with the long-lasting jarred chutneys, pickles and relishes you buy in gourmet stores; those products have been preserved by professionals. Home canning is not something to be undertaken lightly and we are not going to undertake it here.

Think of fresh chutneys and relishes differently: Their freshness is the point—that and the fact that they're prepared quickly (even by novices) using perfectly ordinary kitchen equipment. None of which can be said for home-canned anything.

How Long Will These Things Last Anyway?

That depends. Each recipe includes an estimate of how long the chutney or relish will last (at peak flavor) if it's promptly refrigerated. Some products are tip-top only for a day or two, others will be good for at least a week—especially the ones containing a lot of vinegar and sugar. However, it's impossible to predict the life span without knowing how fresh your ingredients were, how cold your fridge is, how long the chutney sat on the dinner table. The best thing to do is treat the leftovers like any leftovers: refrigerate as soon as possible and discard when they begin to deteriorate.

Storing Your Chutneys and Relishes

Keep your chutneys and relishes in glass jars or plastic containers with tight-fitting lids. Unless you're eating them right away, store them in the refrigerator until serving time and return leftovers to the refrigerator as soon as you reasonably can.

INGREDIENTS

There's nothing out-of-the-ordinary about the ingredients needed for making chutneys and relishes, but a few of them want a word or two of explanation.

Dried Fruit: Look for soft, somewhat plump fruit; avoid hard, dry specimens. Be especially careful when you buy unpackaged dried fruit—that is, dried fruit offered loose at gourmet and health food stores.

Dried herbs (powdered) and spices (ground): Unfortunately, dried herbs and spices lose flavor fairly quickly, so check yours before using. It's best to buy small quantities and keep them in airtight containers.

English-style powdered mustard: There are American brands of powdered mustard, but the English style (Colman's, for example) is nippier.

Fresh herbs: There is no substitute for fresh herbs. Look for unblemished leaves with no withering or yellowing and use them as soon as possible.

Fresh lemon or lime juice: Fresh juice, squeezed from a real lemon or lime, makes an enormous difference in the flavor of a chutney or relish. So don't cheat—no substitutes allowed here.

Fresh pepper: Food, including chutneys and relishes, should be seasoned with freshly ground black pepper, never with preground pepper from a can. Buy black peppercorns by the quarter or half pound and grind them in a pepper grinder as needed.

Garlic: Whole heads of garlic comprise many individual cloves. Be sure yours are firm, with dry papery skin and no sprouting from the stem end.

Ginger: Fresh ginger should be plump and firm, with

a dry light brown skin and no shriveling; peel the skin before using. Wrap leftovers tightly in plastic wrap and store in the refrigerator. You'll also find crystallized and ground ginger used in this book.

Grated lemon or orange rind: To make grated rind, firmly rub the outermost layer of the lemon or orange against the large or small perforations of your metal grater, rotating the fruit as you grate each section. Tap the grater on the counter to dislodge most of the grated rind and then use a pastry brush to push all the remaining bits out.

Hot pepper: The three forms you'll encounter in this book, other than fresh or bottled chiles, are hot red pepper flakes, whole dried red chiles and pure ground chile powder. *Hot red pepper flakes* are flakes of dried red pepper, which can be very hot indeed. Buy the flakes in any food store. *Whole dried red chiles* are small and brittle and generally of unknown provenance—they can be cayenne peppers, bird peppers, Thai peppers or chiles de árbol. They are used as flavoring and are usually removed before serving. Buy them in gourmet stores or in Asian or Latino markets. *Pure ground chile powder* is mild or hot dried chiles ground to a powder—not to be confused with our American chili powder, a ready-made blend of herbs and spices.

Jalapeños: Jalapeño chiles, the most widely available hot peppers, are on the market in at least two forms—

fresh (both green and red) and bottled. The bottled chiles vary greatly in taste: Some are preserved in a mild vinegar brine that keeps the pepper tasting pretty much like itself; others are preserved in a more elaborate pickling liquid, which is also delicious and adds a distinctive flavor to the jalapeños.

Some fresh jalapeños are mild and others are fiery, and the only way to discover which is which is to taste a tiny sliver of the one you're using. If it's very hot, you may want to cut down on the amount you use in a recipe; if it's mild, you may want to add more.

Note: If you have a favorite fresh hot pepper you'd like to substitute for the jalapeño specified in one of the recipes, by all means give it a try.

Light and dark brown sugar: If you don't have one, you can get away with using the other. To measure, pack firmly into your measuring spoon or cup.

Soy sauce: If you have an Asian market nearby, try one of the Chinese brands of regular soy sauce, thin soy sauce or light soy sauce (light in color, not "lite" in sodium). If these are unavailable to you, Kikkoman brand soy sauce is acceptable.

Sun-dried tomatoes: These goodies come in two forms—dry halves sold loose and plump halves packed in oil in jars. The oil-packed tomatoes are considerably more expensive, but are ready to use; the loose tomatoes are a better deal and free of fat, but they can be stiff and salty and must be prepared for use. To do this, rinse them well and simmer for several minutes in a small saucepan of water, until softened. Taste and, if still too salty, repeat with fresh water. Drain and pat dry on paper towels.

Superfine sugar: This is finely granulated sugar that dissolves quickly and easily even in cold liquid. It's sometimes called bar sugar.

Vinegars: Get to know your vinegars. They are quite distinct from each other, and different ones are appropriate for different recipes. Distilled white vinegar is the strongest and harshest; balsamic and cider vinegars have fruity overtones; red and white wine vinegars range from mild to pungent, from winy to just plain acidic; sherry vinegar is mellow and Japanese rice vinegar is mild. You may, on occasion, want to substitute one vinegar for another.

PANTRY

Although you'll undoubtedly have to do a bit of grocery shopping for a few of the ingredients listed in the recipe you choose, some of the necessary ingredients will be ready and waiting in your well-stocked pantry. Here's what you should have:

• Dried herbs and spices (check individual recipes)

- Fresh pepper (black peppercorns in a grinder)
- Garlic cloves
- Honey
- Oils: extra-virgin olive oil; one or two neutral vegetable oils (corn, safflower, canola or sunflower); peanut oil
- Onions (ordinary yellow onions)
- Salt
- Sugar: granulated sugar; light and dark brown sugar; superfine sugar
- Vinegars: balsamic vinegar; cider vinegar; red wine vinegar; white wine vinegar

EQUIPMENT

For making these chutneys and relishes, you'll need basic cooking equipment: a large skillet (12 inches in diameter) with a tight-fitting lid; large, medium and small saucepans with lids; mixing bowls; good knives, including a serrated one; vegetable peeler; metal grater; strainer; colander; glass measuring cups; metal measuring cups and spoons. Many of the recipes also require a food processor, which has acquired the status of basic equipment in the modern kitchen.

Note: Since chutneys and relishes almost always include vinegar or some other acid, they must be cooked in *nonreactive* saucepans and skillets—pans that don't react unpleasantly with acid to create off flavors and peculiar colors. This business of acid reaction was a real problem back when everyone had unanodized aluminum and unlined copper pans, but today—unless you're clinging to the battered aluminum pans you bought when you were in college—you probably don't own a single reactive pan. Your pans should be (and in all likelihood are) made of stainless steel, ceramic, enameled steel or enameled cast iron, tin-lined copper, anodized aluminum or even flameproof glass. All of these are nonreactive.

In addition to these basics, you'll need plastic or glass containers with tight-fitting lids for storing your chutneys and relishes.

TECHNIQUES

Cooking technique is not a major issue in these recipes. If you can chop, dice, mince and stir, you can make chutneys and relishes. There are, however, three pieces of information that may be useful if you don't already know them.

How to Handle Hot Peppers

Hot peppers (chiles), such as jalapeños, habañeros, serranos and bird peppers, are hot because the central cores, veins and seeds contain a powerful chemical called capsaicin. Capsaicin is so strong that it can give you second-degree burns if you come in direct contact with it, but more commonly it will just sting your hands for hours, in spite of all the scrubbing you may do. You might even notice that when you cut up a hot pepper, the air around you irritates your nose and throat. Be smart: Wear rubber gloves when you prep and mince hot peppers and never touch your eyes, nose or lips. Wash the gloves with soap and water when you're done.

How to Stem, Halve, Seed and Devein a Pepper

This technique is the same for fresh bell peppers, mild chiles and hot peppers.

Using a small sharp knife, cut around the stem of your pepper and lift out the stem and central core. Cut the pepper in half lengthwise. Tap the pepper on the counter to dislodge most of the seeds and brush out the rest with your fingers. (If you prefer, rinse out the seeds and then pat the pepper dry on paper towels.) Use the knife to cut out the light-colored veins (also called ribs).

Note: Bottled hot peppers are prepared a little differently. Simply slice off the stem end of the pepper, slit lengthwise and pull out the central core and stringy veins. Rinse out the seeds and pat the pepper dry on paper towels.

How to Roast a Fresh Pepper

The procedure, if you have a gas range, is simple: Impale the pepper on a long kitchen fork, pushing the tines into the stem end. Hold the pepper over a medium flame, turning it as each area chars and blackens. If necessary, reposition the pepper on the fork to allow the flame to reach all parts of the pepper. Put the completely charred pepper in a colander in the sink; do *not* paper-bag it, as this steams and overcooks the pepper.

Run cold water over the pepper, rubbing off the blackened skin; the colander will catch all the charred bits. Pat dry and use according to the recipe instructions.

Important: The roasting procedure is exactly the same for bell peppers, mild chiles and hot peppers, except that the skin of the mild chiles and hot peppers is thinner and takes very little time to char. More important, you must protect your hands by wearing rubber gloves when you rub off the charred skin.

If you have an electric range, roast your peppers under the broiler, turning them as they char.

Fruit Chutneys and Relishes

Some fresh fruits—cranberries, for instance—seem to have been put on this earth for the sole purpose of becoming condiments. Other fruits, usually enjoyed in their natural states, are so adaptable that they can easily have second careers as chutneys and relishes: Apples, peaches and plums come immediately to mind. And there's a third group (including bananas, pineapples, and melons), whose versatility you'd never guess, that can be made into wonderful condiments.

There's a subgroup, too: luscious dried fruits such as raisins, dates, figs, apricots, cherries and even blueberries. Keep in mind that both dried fruits and fresh ones make delicious chutneys and relishes, though of quite different styles. The dried fruits have more concentrated flavors and hold up well with generous hits of spices, herbs and other punchy seasonings. Fresh fruits generally require a lighter touch when flavorings are added; the goal is to produce an interesting condiment without losing the flavor of the fresh fruit.

There are new combinations of fruits among the recipes, as well as traditional ones you may not have tasted before. Be adventurous.

Tangy Cantaloupe Relish

Makes about 3 ½ cups   Here's a fruit relish with an unexpected spin—sweet juicy cantaloupe combined with savory lime juice, chives and peppers. It's a great way to take advantage of plentiful seasonal melons and a nice change from the usual wedge on a plate.

M E N U   S U G G E S T I O N S

Delicious alongside cold sliced ham or smoked pork, with herb-and-garlic-seasoned veal roast or with grilled marinated chicken. For a meatless meal, serve the relish with shrimp, scallops or crab, a simple green salad and plenty of crusty bread.

2 TABLESPOONS FRESH LIME JUICE

2 TABLESPOONS WATER

2 TEASPOONS SUPERFINE SUGAR

1 TABLESPOON SNIPPED CHIVES OR MINCED SCALLION (GREEN PART ONLY)

SALT AND FRESHLY GROUND PEPPER

1 MEDIUM-SIZE RIPE CANTALOUPE

½ FRESH OR BOTTLED JALAPEÑO

1 SMALL OR ½ MEDIUM-SIZE RED BELL PEPPER

1. In a large bowl, combine the lime juice, water, sugar, chives and a good sprinkling of salt and pepper. Whisk until the sugar dissolves.

2. Use a serrated knife to peel the cantaloupe, making sure to remove the green layer beneath the scaly skin.

Cut the melon in half and scoop out the seeds and strings. Cut the flesh in ½-inch cubes and add them to the bowl.

3. Stem, seed and devein the jalapeño; mince and add it to the bowl. Stem, halve, seed and devein the bell pepper; cut it in 1-inch strips, then cut the strips cross-wise in slivers. Add the bell pepper to the bowl and stir well. Taste the relish and add more salt and pepper if needed.

Let the relish marinate in the refrigerator for 1 hour, stirring occasionally.

Serve the relish slightly chilled but not icy.

This relish should be prepared and eaten on the same day. It's a fresh relish, not a long-lasting one.

Honeydew-Starfruit Relish

Makes about 4 cups This is perfect for late summer and early fall, when honeydew melons are widely available. I love the contrast between the sweet succulent melon and the crisp, lemony starfruit.

MENU SUGGESTIONS

The recipe makes a large amount of relish, so try it as a bed for a beautiful grilled or baked whole fish (such as pompano or red snapper) or for grilled or broiled bluefish fillets. At brunch, offer the relish with pan-fried Canadian bacon or sausages and French toast or a sweet bread pudding.

GRATED RIND AND JUICE OF
  1 LEMON
1 TABLESPOON EXTRA-VIRGIN
  OLIVE OIL
1 TEASPOON FINELY MINCED
  FRESH GINGER
⅛ TEASPOON POWDERED
  THYME
⅛ TEASPOON POWDERED
  ROSEMARY

2 PINCHES OF SALT
1 SMALL RIPE OR ALMOST-
  RIPE HONEYDEW MELON
1 MEDIUM-SIZE RIPE STAR-
  FRUIT (ABOUT ½ POUND, 5
  INCHES LONG; SEE NOTE)
MINCED OR WHOLE FRESH
  MINT LEAVES FOR GARNISH
  (OPTIONAL)

1. In a large bowl, whisk together the grated rind, lemon juice (no seeds, please), olive oil, ginger, herbs and salt.
2. Halve the melon and scoop out the seeds and strings. Cut the ripe flesh away from the rind and dice

enough of the flesh to make 3 cups. Add the diced melon to the large bowl.

Cut off and discard about half an inch from each end of the starfruit. Cut the starfruit crosswise in ⅛-inch slices, picking out and discarding any seeds from the centers. Add the slices to the large bowl.

3. Stir the fruit mixture gently but thoroughly and allow it to marinate for an hour in the refrigerator, stirring occasionally. Transfer to a serving bowl or platter and, if you like, sprinkle with mint.

Serve slightly chilled or keep the relish in the refrigerator until about half an hour before needed and serve it at room temperature.

Although it lasts for 2 days in the refrigerator, it's best to eat this relish as soon as possible. After the second day it loses distinction.

Note: Starfruit, which is also called carambola, may be new to you. Look for golden yellow fruit with shiny, unblemished skin; wash it well and store in the refrigerator. If the skin is greenish, let the fruit ripen first at room temperature. Starfruit is not peeled before using, but you may want to pare off the dark brown edges.

Cranberry-Currant Relish

Makes about 3 cups This is deep and rich, not overly sweet, with a delicious winy overtaste. This relish is certainly not just for Thanksgiving, but keep the recipe in mind when it's your turn to bring the cranberries.

MENU SUGGESTIONS
Roasted turkey, of course, but great with roasted chicken and duck, too, as well as pork and ham. For a vegetarian meal, try it with a wild mushroom ragout, a grain casserole and green beans with dill.

½ CUP DRIED CURRANTS
½ CUP PORT
1 CUP CURRANT JELLY
2 TABLESPOONS BALSAMIC
  OR CIDER VINEGAR
¼ CUP WATER
1 TABLESPOON MINCED
  FRESH GINGER

1 TEASPOON DRAINED PRE-
  PARED HORSERADISH
4 CUPS (ABOUT 1 POUND)
  FRESH CRANBERRIES
PINCH OF SALT
¼ CUP SUGAR

1. Combine the currants and port in a jar or plastic container, cover and let the currants soak for at least 1 hour. Don't worry about soaking them too long—let them get good and tipsy.
2. Meanwhile, in a large saucepan melt the currant jelly with the vinegar and water. Stir in the ginger, horseradish, cranberries and salt and simmer uncov-

ered for about 20 minutes, stirring often, until most of the cranberries have burst and there is no liquid left.

3. Add the currants, port and sugar and simmer uncovered for 1 more minute, stirring constantly. Let the relish cool until it is just warm, stirring occasionally to release heat.

While it's still warm, spoon the relish into a bowl or small mold to finish cooling either at room temperature or in the refrigerator. The relish will jell as it cools, so when it's completely cool you may either serve it from the bowl or turn it out onto a plate.

Serve right away or cover well and refrigerate until needed.

The relish will last for at least a week in the refrigerator (although it tends to get a little bitter toward the end of the week), so you may make it ahead.

Gingered Cranberry-

Makes about 2½ cups Dried cranberries (rather than fresh ones) are combined with juicy oranges to make this spicy-sweet relish to go with the Thanksgiving bird or with any appropriate company dinner.

M E N U   S U G G E S T I O N S

Great with baked ham or crown roast of pork, roasted duck or venison. This relish gives a special lift to holiday leftovers—it's perfect alongside a hot turkey sandwich with gravy. For a savory breakfast or brunch, spoon the relish onto waffles, pancakes or French toast, and serve with turkey sausage or chicken hash,

¾ CUP ORANGE JUICE
GRATED RIND OF 1 LEMON
PINCH OF GROUND ALL-
   SPICE
PINCH OF GROUND CLOVES
1 CUP (ABOUT 5 OUNCES)
   DRIED CRANBERRIES
¼ CUP MINCED OR FINELY
   CHOPPED ONION
3 MEDIUM NAVEL ORANGES
1 OUNCE CRYSTALLIZED
   GINGER
½ TABLESPOON SWEET OR
   SALTED BUTTER
SALT

Orange Relish

1. In a medium saucepan, stir together the orange juice, grated lemon rind, spices, cranberries and onion. Bring to a simmer, cover and continue cooking over low heat for 5 minutes, until the cranberries are soft and the liquid is reduced by about half.

2. Meanwhile, use either a sharp straight-bladed knife or a serrated knife to remove the peel from the oranges, making sure to cut away all the bitter white pith. Halve the oranges, remove the white fibers from the center and cut the flesh in ½-inch slices. Julienne the ginger.

3. Add the oranges, ginger, butter and a sprinkling of salt to the saucepan and stir gently to melt the butter while keeping the orange slices intact. Let the relish cool, then add a little more salt if needed.

Serve right away at room temperature or refrigerate until slightly chilled. If you make it ahead, keep the relish refrigerated until close to serving time.

It's best to make and eat this relish on the same day. It will last into a second day, but not longer.

Spiced Pear Chutney

Makes about 2½ cups I like to make this lemon-spiked chutney in autumn or winter when pears are plentiful and tasty. The texture here is especially appealing, the tender diced pears and raisins making a nice contrast with the crunchy pecans.

MENU SUGGESTIONS

Pear chutney works well with flavorful roasts such as pork or veal prepared with plenty of fresh herbs—rosemary, oregano, sage. It's great with roasted poultry, too. Vegetarians might like to serve the chutney with a savory cheese bread pudding and a green salad.

4 FIRM-RIPE BOSC PEARS (1½ TO 1¾ POUNDS); ANJOU OR BARTLETT PEARS MAY BE SUBSTITUTED
⅓ CUP GOLDEN RAISINS
⅓ CUP CHOPPED PECANS
GRATED RIND OF 1 LEMON
1 TABLESPOON FRESH LEMON JUICE
⅓ CUP CIDER VINEGAR
⅓ CUP PACKED LIGHT BROWN SUGAR
⅛ TEASPOON CINNAMON
⅛ TEASPOON GROUND GINGER
⅛ TEASPOON NUTMEG
SALT

1. Peel, quarter and core the pears, making sure to remove all the seeds and hard matter. Cut the pears in small dice or chop them in pea-size pieces.

with Pecans

2. Put all the ingredients, including the pears and a sprinkling of salt, in a medium saucepan and bring to a simmer, uncovered, stirring to dissolve the sugar.

Cover the saucepan and simmer over low heat for 20 minutes, stirring occasionally. Uncover the pan and continue cooking over low heat for 20 more minutes, stirring occasionally. The pears should be tender and any remaining liquid should be syrupy.

Let the chutney cool.

Serve right away at room temperature or refrigerate until about half an hour before needed—the taste is best when the chutney is room temperature or cool, but not cold.

This chutney lasts at least a week in the refrigerator.

Pear–Hot Pepper

Makes about 2½ cups Certain fruits and vegetables were made for each other—pears and red bell pepper are a perfect example. In this savory-sweet chutney they're combined with hot pepper, ginger and coriander seeds.

Tip: As the days go by, the coriander seeds soften in the chutney and become rather pungent, so if you're not a big coriander fan, either eat the chutney within a day or two or leave the coriander seeds out.

MENU SUGGESTIONS

Spread this on ham, turkey or cheese sandwiches. Serve with chili (beef, pork or vegetable) and corn bread, with baked or broiled chicken, with chicken tacos or tostadas. For a meatless meal, the chutney is wonderful with a savory spinach-feta pie or a curried broccoli tart. It's also nice at lunch or brunch with cheese quesadillas, sliced avocado and a black bean salad.

4 FIRM-RIPE ANJOU PEARS (1½ TO 1¾ POUNDS) (OR BOSC OR BARTLETT PEARS)
1 FRESH JALAPEÑO
1 SMALL GARLIC CLOVE
½ RED BELL PEPPER
½ TEASPOON CORIANDER SEEDS

1 TEASPOON MINCED FRESH GINGER
⅓ CUP PACKED LIGHT BROWN SUGAR
⅓ CUP CIDER VINEGAR
SALT

Chutney

1. Peel, quarter and core the pears, making sure to remove all the seeds and hard matter. Cut the pears in small dice or chop them in pea-size pieces.

Stem, halve, seed and devein the jalapeño. Mince the jalapeño, garlic and bell pepper.

2. Put all the ingredients, including a sprinkling of salt, in a medium saucepan and bring to a simmer, uncovered, stirring to dissolve the sugar.

Cover the saucepan and simmer over low heat for 20 minutes, then uncover and continue cooking over low heat for 20 more minutes. The pears should be tender and any liquid left should be syrupy.

Let the chutney cool, then add a little more salt if needed.

Serve right away at room temperature or refrigerate until half an hour before needed, so the chutney is slightly chilled but not icy.

This chutney is best on the first and second day, but is still quite good for another 2 or 3 days.

Tipsy Dried-Apple

Makes about 2½ cups Deep and dark in color, this delicious chutney has a woodsy, earthy flavor. And no, there's no mistake in the ingredients list—you'll need 1 cup of sherry plus 2 cups of red wine for this recipe. That's what makes the chutney both tipsy and special.

M E N U   S U G G E S T I O N S
Delicious with venison, roast beef or beef bourguignonne; with grilled or pan-fried sausage—chicken, turkey, pork or veal; with any sort of roasted bird. Or serve the chutney with pan-fried slices of polenta, a chunk of sharp cheese and plenty of crisp green vegetables.

2 CUPS PACKED DRIED AP-
  PLES (ABOUT 6 OUNCES)
¼ CUP DRIED CURRANTS
¼ CUP CHOPPED WALNUTS
1 CUP SWEET SHERRY
  (*OLOROSO,* ALSO CALLED
  CREAM OR GOLDEN
  SHERRY)
½ CUP APPLE JUICE OR WA-
  TER

2 CUPS RED WINE
¼ CUP SHERRY VINEGAR
¼ CUP PACKED DARK BROWN
  SUGAR
½ TEASPOON FRESHLY
  GROUND PEPPER
⅛ TEASPOON SALT

Chutney

1. Using a scissors or sharp knife, cut the apples in small dice, discarding any hard bits of core or skin that may have been left when the apples were dried.

2. Combine all the ingredients, including the apples, in a medium saucepan. Bring to a simmer and continue simmering uncovered over low heat, stirring often, for 30 minutes. The apples will be very soft and a deep wine-red color and the liquid will be almost completely gone.

Let the chutney cool.

Serve warm or at room temperature or, if you prefer, slightly chilled. If you've made it ahead, refrigerate the chutney until about half an hour before serving.

The chutney will last for at least a week in the refrigerator.

Apple-Chile Relish

Makes about 2½ cups Apples and peppers, like pears and peppers, have a natural affinity for each other. This lightly cooked relish contains roasted mild chile and chewy carrot to give it texture, and jalapeño and onion for a bit of kick.

M E N U   S U G G E S T I O N S

I like this with barbecued beef or broiled steak (hot or cold), with barbecued or baked spareribs, with braised pork chops. Also good on a ham, roast beef or meat loaf sandwich for lunch. For brunch, serve this relish with a cheese omelet and corn muffins. Try it with cornmeal-fried fish fillets (grouper, snapper or cod); vegetarians can have it with vegetable tacos or with melted cheddar cheese sandwiches.

2 LARGE OR 3 MEDIUM
  GRANNY SMITH OR OTHER
  TART-SWEET APPLES (1 TO
  1¼ POUNDS)
1 MEDIUM CARROT
1 FRESH MILD GREEN CHILE
  (POBLANO, ANAHEIM, ETC.)

2 PICKLED JALAPEÑOS
¼ CUP CIDER VINEGAR
¼ CUP WATER
¼ CUP SUGAR
¼ TEASPOON SALT
1 GARLIC CLOVE, MINCED
¼ CUP MINCED RED ONION

1. Peel, quarter and core the apples, making sure to re-move all the seeds and hard matter from the centers. Cut the apples in small dice or chop them in pea-size pieces.

Trim, peel and grate the carrot.

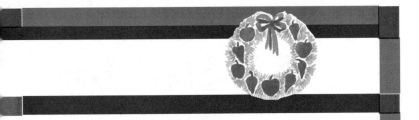

2. Roast the fresh chile (see How to Roast a Fresh Pepper, page 22) and rub off the charred skin. Stem, halve, seed and devein the chile and julienne the flesh.

Stem, halve and seed the pickled jalapeños; mince.

3. In a medium saucepan, combine the vinegar, water, sugar, salt and garlic. Bring to a simmer, stirring to dissolve the sugar. Add the apples, stir well and continue simmering uncovered for 10 minutes, until the apples are tender.

4. Stir the grated carrot into the apple mixture and continue cooking, stirring constantly, for 1 minute. There should be only a little liquid left in the saucepan. Turn off the heat.

5. Stir the roasted chile, pickled jalapeños and minced onion into the apple mixture.

Let the relish cool, then season with more salt if needed.

Serve immediately at room temperature or serve slightly chilled. If you make it ahead, refrigerate the relish until about half an hour before serving.

This relish will keep well for 3 days in the refrigerator, getting hotter each day.

Savory Apple-Onion

Makes about 3½ cups I've been making this savory-sweet chutney, with slight variations, for a good twenty years. It's the first chutney I ever ate and the one that showed me there was more to condiments than dill pickles.

MENU SUGGESTIONS

Try this with roasted chicken or sautéed chicken breasts, with roasted lamb, with a warm duck salad on greens or with all kinds of cold cuts and cold meats, including pâtés. It's great on a cold meat loaf sandwich, too. For a meatless meal, serve the chutney with a root vegetable stew, lentils and plenty of basmati rice.

2 LARGE OR 3 MEDIUM
GRANNY SMITH OR OTHER
TART-SWEET APPLES (1 TO
1¼ POUNDS)
1 LARGE OR 2 MEDIUM
ONIONS
2 TABLESPOONS NEUTRAL
VEGETABLE OIL (CORN, SAF-
FLOWER, CANOLA OR SUN-
FLOWER)
1 TEASPOON MINCED FRESH
GINGER
1 GARLIC CLOVE, MINCED
½ TEASPOON MILD CURRY
POWDER

⅛ TEASPOON CINNAMON
⅛ TEASPOON GROUND
CLOVES
1 TABLESPOON YELLOW MUS-
TARD SEEDS
½ CUP DARK RAISINS
½ CUP PACKED LIGHT BROWN
SUGAR
¾ CUP CIDER
VINEGAR
¼ CUP WATER
¼ TEASPOON
SALT

Chutney

1. Peel, quarter and core the apples, making sure to re-move all the seeds and hard matter. Cut the apples in small dice or chop them in pea-size pieces.

Chop the onion.

2. In a medium saucepan, heat the oil and sauté the ginger and garlic over low heat for about 1 minute. Add the curry powder, spices and mustard seeds and continue sautéing and stirring for another minute.

3. Add the onions, raisins, brown sugar, vinegar, water and salt and stir well. Bring the mixture to a simmer, stirring to dissolve the sugar, then lower the heat slightly and continue simmering uncovered for 25 min-utes.

Stir in the apples and simmer uncovered for 20 more minutes, until the mixture is very thick and there is no liquid left. If there is liquid left, turn up the heat and boil it off, stirring constantly for 1 or 2 minutes.

Let the chutney cool.

Serve at room temperature or cool (but not cold). If you make the chutney ahead, refrigerate until about half an hour before serving.

Savory Apple-Onion Chutney will last at least a week in the refrigerator.

Lemon-Quince Relish

Makes about 2½ cups Raw quince, not your everyday fruit, tastes rather like an unripe pear crossed with a tart-sweet apple. The texture of the raw fruit is grainy and hard, but when quince is cooked it becomes tender and mellow, with a delicately sweet flavor.

Tip: Ripe quinces are firm and golden yellow (not green), and they may have some pale grayish fuzz still clinging to the skin.

M E N U   S U G G E S T I O N S
Quince relish makes a nice contrast with rich meat (such as pork roast) but also complements a more subtly flavored veal roast or roasted Cornish hen. For breakfast or brunch, this relish is good with a sweet omelet or on French toast made with brioche, with fresh raspberries. Vegetarians might like to try the relish with squash pie, collard greens and a dish of braised chestnuts.

3 RIPE QUINCES (1¼ TO 1½ POUNDS)
⅓ CUP SUGAR
½ CUP WATER
2 TABLESPOONS JAPANESE RICE VINEGAR
GRATED RIND AND JUICE OF 1 LEMON
1 TEASPOON FINELY MINCED FRESH GINGER
⅓ CUP DRIED CURRANTS
SALT

1. Cut off the top and bottom of each quince and peel the fruit. Cut in quarters and core as you would an apple, making sure to remove all the hard matter and seeds. Cut in slices and then chop in pea-size bits.

2. Put the sugar, water, vinegar, grated rind, lemon juice and ginger in a medium saucepan and bring to a simmer, stirring to dissolve the sugar. Continue simmering uncovered for 5 minutes.

3. Add the quince, currants and a dash of salt and stir well. Cover the saucepan and continue cooking over low heat for 7 minutes; uncover the pan and simmer for 3 more minutes, until the quince is quite tender and the liquid is almost gone.

Let the relish cool.

Serve at room temperature or slightly chilled. If you make the relish ahead, refrigerate until about half an hour before serving.

The relish will last for at least a week in the refrigerator.

Nippy Lemon Chutney

Makes about 2½ cups A real lemon-lover's delight—tangy, biting, sweet, sour and even a little bitter. This chutney is about as lemony as a condiment can get. It may remind you of lemon marmalade, except for the garlic and jalapeño.

M E N U   S U G G E S T I O N S

Lemon chutney livens up simple fish dishes such as poached salmon or trout, sautéed fillets of flounder, sole or turbot. It's great with crab or lobster salad, salmon croquettes, shrimp or scallops en brochette, especially served on a bed of soft greens. If you're not a fish fan, try the chutney with sautéed chicken breasts or roasted chicken leg quarters. Whole-wheat couscous goes well with any of these.

1 CUP SUGAR	1 TABLESPOON MINCED
1 CUP DISTILLED WHITE	FRESH GINGER
VINEGAR	2 GARLIC CLOVES, MINCED
5 PERFECT LEMONS	1 TEASPOON SALT
1 FRESH JALAPEÑO	FRESHLY GROUND PEPPER

1. Combine the sugar and vinegar in a medium saucepan and bring to a simmer, stirring to dissolve the sugar. Continue simmering over medium heat for about 15 minutes, until reduced by half, to make a hot syrup.

2. Meanwhile, quarter the lemons lengthwise. Cut out

the white fiber from the center of each quarter. Cut each quarter in half crosswise and—this is important—remove all the seeds.

Put the pieces of lemon in your food processor and pulse until the lemons are chopped in small pieces.

Stem, halve, seed and devein the jalapeño; mince.

3. Add the lemons, minced jalapeño, ginger, garlic, salt and several grinds of fresh pepper to the hot syrup and bring to a simmer. Continue simmering uncovered over medium heat for about 15 minutes, until the lemon peel is tender but not mushy.

4. Turn the lemon mixture out into a strainer set over a bowl. Set the lemons (in the strainer) aside and pour the liquid in the bowl back into the saucepan. Simmer the liquid over low heat until it is reduced to a very thick brown syrup. Stir the lemons into the thick syrup.

Let the chutney cool.

Serve at room temperature or chilled. If you make the chutney ahead, keep it refrigerated until about half an hour before serving.

Tightly covered, this chutney will last for at least 2 weeks in the refrigerator.

Fresh Orange—

Makes about 2½ cups This relish is bright, juicy and quite sweet, with a gingery flavor and plenty of crunch.

Tip: Try the relish as a topping for vanilla frozen yogurt or ice cream. Sensational!

M E N U   S U G G E S T I O N S
This is a fine accompaniment for pork, ham or duck, as well as simple baked or roasted chicken or Cornish hens. Try the relish with a selection of sausages—sweet or hot Italian sausage, spicy chorizo, chicken or turkey sausage with herbs, veal sausage. At breakfast or brunch, serve with omelets filled with a creamy herb cheese (Boursin, for example) or over ricotta-stuffed crêpes. Vegetarians can match the relish with corn fritters and a green salad with crumbled blue cheese.

3 MEDIUM NAVEL ORANGES
½ CUP ORANGE JUICE
⅔ CUP DICED DRIED APRICOTS
1 TABLESPOON CHOPPED CRYSTALLIZED GINGER

¼ CUP SUGAR
3 TABLESPOONS HONEY
PINCH OF SALT
½ CUP CHOPPED WALNUTS

1. Grate the rind of one orange and combine the grated rind in a medium saucepan with the orange

Walnut Relish

juice, apricots, ginger, sugar, honey and salt. Simmer the mixture uncovered for about 5 minutes, until there is only a little syrupy liquid left in the pan along with the softened apricots.

2. Meanwhile, peel the oranges using either a sharp straight-bladed knife or a serrated knife, making sure to cut away all the bitter white pith.

Cut the oranges in half and then in quarters; remove the white fiber from the centers. Cut the oranges in ½-inch chunks. Gently stir the orange chunks and the walnuts into the hot syrup in the saucepan. Let the relish cool, stirring occasionally to release heat and to incorporate the juice exuded by the warm orange chunks.

Refrigerate the relish and serve chilled.

The relish will last for about a week in the refrigerator.

Sweet Ripe Mango

Makes about 2½ cups This chutney is a particular favorite of mine, in part because I love the smooth, firm texture of the cooked mango. The finished chutney is lightly spicy, with soft plump raisins and slivered almonds to add textural interest.

MENU SUGGESTIONS

Serve with curry, of course—chicken, lamb, beef or vegetable. Also great with lemon chicken, with leg of lamb, with broiled sirloin steak, with broiled swordfish steak or sautéed shrimp. For a meatless meal, offer the chutney with Indian-style vegetarian dishes featuring potatoes and spinach, eggplant, cauliflower, lentils.

½ CUP DISTILLED WHITE VINEGAR
¼ CUP WATER
½ CUP SUGAR
1 GARLIC CLOVE, MINCED
1 TABLESPOON JULIENNED FRESH GINGER
1 TEASPOON YELLOW MUSTARD SEEDS

1 TEASPOON GRATED ORANGE RIND
¼ TEASPOON HOT RED PEPPER FLAKES
SALT
2 FIRM-RIPE MANGOES
½ CUP DARK RAISINS
½ CUP SLIVERED BLANCHED ALMONDS

1. In a medium saucepan, stir together the vinegar, water, sugar, garlic, ginger, mustard seeds, orange rind,

Chutney with Nuts

pepper flakes and a pinch or two of salt. Bring to a simmer, stirring to dissolve the sugar, and continue simmering uncovered over medium-low heat for about 15 minutes, until syrupy.

2. Meanwhile, peel the mangoes and cut the flesh from the pits. Slice the flesh about ¼ inch thick and cut each slice in half lengthwise and then crosswise to make short strips.

Add the pieces of mango to the hot syrup and simmer uncovered over low heat for 15 minutes.

3. Stir the raisins and almonds into the mango mixture and continue to simmer uncovered over low heat for 5 more minutes until the fruit and nuts are coated in a thick syrup. Add a little more salt if needed and let the chutney cool.

Serve at room temperature or cool. If you make the chutney ahead, keep it refrigerated until about half an hour before needed.

This chutney will last for at least a week in the refrigerator.

Hot Green Mango

Makes about 3½ cups Even green (unripe) mangoes have a light sweetness that gives an appealing undertone to the complex herbs and seasonings of this chutney.

Remember, this chutney is supposed to be hot, but you may certainly cut down on the amount of jalapeño if it seems a bit too much for you.

M E N U   S U G G E S T I O N S

As with sweet mango chutney, hot mango chutney is delicious with curries of all kinds, as well as simpler dishes of roasted chicken, beef or lamb. It's also wonderful with sautéed fish fillets (mackerel or snapper, for instance) and shrimp in almost any form. I like to serve the chutney with plenty of basmati rice and a cool raita.

2 GREEN (UNRIPE) MANGOES
1 SMALL ONION
2 FRESH JALAPEÑOS
2 TABLESPOONS NEUTRAL VEGETABLE OIL (CORN, SAFFLOWER, CANOLA OR SUNFLOWER)
⅛ TEASPOON GROUND CUMIN
⅛ TEASPOON FENNEL SEEDS
⅛ TEASPOON CORIANDER SEEDS
2 TEASPOONS YELLOW MUSTARD SEEDS

1 WHOLE DRIED RED CHILE
1½ TABLESPOONS MINCED FRESH GINGER
2 TEASPOONS MINCED GARLIC
⅓ CUP CIDER VINEGAR
⅓ CUP WATER
⅓ CUP ROASTED UNSALTED PUMPKIN SEEDS
SALT

Chutney

1. Peel the mangoes, cut the flesh from the pits and slice the flesh ¼ inch thick. Cut each slice in half crosswise.

Quarter the onion and slice it ⅛ inch thick. Stem, halve, seed and devein the jalapeños; slice them crosswise as thin as possible.

2. In a large skillet, heat the vegetable oil and sauté the cumin, fennel seeds, coriander seeds, mustard seeds and dried red chile for 10 seconds. Add the ginger and garlic and sauté for 1 minute.

3. Add the vinegar and water and simmer for 1 minute. Add the mangoes, onions, jalapeño and pumpkin seeds and simmer uncovered for 5 minutes, stirring often, until the mangoes are firm-tender and there is

only a little liquid left. Remove the whole red pepper, add salt to taste and let the chutney cool.

Serve the chutney at room temperature or slightly chilled. If you've made the chutney ahead, keep it refrigerated until about half an hour before serving.

This chutney will last about a week in the refrigerator.

Green Papaya Relish

Makes about 2 cups Green (unripe) papayas are used in the Caribbean, in Southeast Asia and other parts of the world for making condiments. Although many unripe fruits are hard and sour, green papaya has a smooth texture and a bland, slightly sweet taste that is used to advantage in this bright, citrusy relish. (In fact, when it's unripe, papaya hasn't yet acquired the characteristic taste that some people dislike.)

MENU SUGGESTIONS

Great with Thai-style and Caribbean-style dishes (homemade or take-out) as well as with sautéed shrimp, pan-seared fresh tuna and other fish fillets. Try the relish with baked marinated chicken or chicken with peanut sauce, too. If you prefer a vegetarian meal, serve the relish with cornmeal-coated pan-fried okra, baked plantains, baked eggplant and sliced tomatoes.

1 GREEN PAPAYA (ABOUT 1 POUND)	1 TEASPOON MINCED FRESH JALAPEÑO
½ TEASPOON SALT	1 TEASPOON MINCED GARLIC
⅓ CUP SLIVERED RED ONION	¼ CUP FRESH LIME JUICE

1. Trim and peel the papaya; halve it lengthwise and scoop out all the strings and black seeds. Grate the flesh on the largest holes of your metal grater or chunk the flesh and grate it in your food processor.

Put the grated papaya in a large bowl, sprinkle with the salt and mix well. Set aside to soften for 30 minutes.

2. Add the remaining ingredients to the bowl and stir well.

Serve right away at room temperature or serve it a bit chilled. Keep the relish refrigerated if you've made it ahead, and take it out about half an hour before serving.

This relish will last for at least 3 days in the refrigerator.

Red Banana Chutney

Makes about 2 cups Red bananas are sweet and firm when ripe—firmer than yellow bananas. If you can't find red bananas, use firm-ripe (not fully ripe) yellow bananas. In this tangy-sweet chutney, most of the ingredients are cooked before the bananas are added; the bananas are simmered only briefly, to soften them and to allow their flavor to marry with the other ingredients.

MENU SUGGESTIONS

Banana chutney will dress up any simple or spicy chicken dish, pork in almost any form (chops, sliced cold roast, etc.), and baked ham. Fish-lovers can serve it with baked or grilled whole fish or fillets—mahimahi, snapper, salmon, sea trout or cod. Try it with poached fish escabèche and a dish of peas and rice in the Caribbean style.

2 TABLESPOONS PEANUT OIL
(OR OTHER VEGETABLE OIL,
EXCEPT OLIVE OIL)
1 SMALL ONION, CHOPPED
1 TABLESPOON MINCED
FRESH GINGER
2 TABLESPOONS FRESH LIME
JUICE
¼ CUP JAPANESE RICE VINE-
GAR

¼ CUP ORANGE JUICE
¼ CUP HONEY
SALT
5 RED BANANAS (ABOUT 1¼
POUNDS)
2 TEASPOONS MINCED FRESH
OR BOTTLED JALAPEÑO
2 TABLESPOONS MINCED
FRESH CORIANDER

with Coriander

1. In a large skillet, heat the oil and brown the onion slowly over medium-low heat. Add the ginger, lime juice, vinegar, orange juice, honey and a sprinkling of salt. Stir well and simmer uncovered over low heat for 10 minutes.

2. Meanwhile, peel and dice the bananas. Add the bananas and minced jalapeño to the vinegar mixture. Stir over low heat for 2 minutes; the liquid should be syrupy and the mixture should be thick. Let the chutney cool completely, then stir in the minced coriander.

Serve right away at room temperature or, if you prefer, slightly chilled. If you make the chutney ahead, keep it refrigerated until about half an hour before serving.

This chutney will last for 3 to 4 days in the refrigerator.

Rich Banana-Raisin

Makes about 2½ cups This sweet chutney is a favorite of mine, with its complex blend of herbs and spices and its rich combination of fruit. As is traditional in India, the herb-spice mixture is heated in oil to bring out the delicate aromas.

MENU SUGGESTIONS
Serve with sautéed chicken or turkey cutlets or with marinated baked chicken thighs or leg quarters. If you prefer meat, try the chutney with roasted lamb or pork. This chutney also complements steamed or baked whole fish.

4 MEDIUM-SIZE FIRM-RIPE BANANAS
1 LARGE GRANNY SMITH APPLE
½ TEASPOON CUMIN SEEDS
½ TEASPOON CORIANDER SEEDS
2 TABLESPOONS NEUTRAL VEGETABLE OIL (CORN, SAFFLOWER, CANOLA OR SUNFLOWER)
FRESHLY GROUND PEPPER
¼ TEASPOON GROUND CLOVES
¼ TEASPOON CINNAMON
¼ TEASPOON TURMERIC
1 TABLESPOON MINCED GARLIC
1 TABLESPOON MINCED FRESH GINGER
½ CUP DARK OR GOLDEN RAISINS
¼ CUP CIDER VINEGAR
2 TABLESPOONS SUGAR
¼ CUP WATER
SALT

1. Peel the bananas and cut them in small dice. Peel, quarter and core the apple, making sure to remove all the seeds and hard matter. Grate the apple on the largest holes of a metal grater

Chutney

2. Crush the cumin and coriander seeds together. In a medium saucepan, heat the oil. Add the cumin, coriander, a few grinds of fresh pepper and the spices and stir over low heat for 2 minutes. Be careful not to let the mixture smoke or burn.Add the garlic and ginger and sauté for 2 more minutes.

3. Turn off the heat. Add the raisins, vinegar, sugar and water to the saucepan; stir well. Bring to a simmer and continue cooking over low heat for 5 minutes, until the sugar dissolves and the raisins are soft.

4. Put the contents of the saucepan into your food processor and pulse several times to make a coarse puree, scraping down the sides of the bowl if necessary. Return the puree to the saucepan.

5. Bring the raisin puree to a simmer, add the bananas, apples and a sprinkling of salt and stir well. Continue simmering, stirring constantly, for 2 minutes, until the apples and bananas soften.

Let the chutney cool.

Serve immediately, warm or at room temperature, or keep the chutney refrigerated and bring it to room temperature before serving.

This chutney lasts for only 2 days, so eat it soon.

Spicy Pineapple Chutney

Makes about 2½ cups Browning the onions and cooking down the sweet pineapple juice give this chutney a caramelized flavor which combines beautifully with the red wine vinegar, honey and cinnamon. Cayenne and freshly ground black pepper add delicious afterburn.

Menu Suggestions

A wonderful accompaniment for roasted chicken, Cornish hens or turkey, for baked or pan-fried ham, for stir-fried pork on rice, for country-style spareribs. If you prefer a meatless meal, try pineapple chutney with bluefish, mackerel, crab cakes or salmon, along with a hearty grain pilaf.

2 TABLESPOONS EXTRA-VIR- GIN OLIVE OIL	¼ TEASPOON CINNAMON
	¼ TEASPOON CAYENNE
1 LARGE ONION, DICED	¼ TEASPOON SALT
1 LARGE RIPE PINEAPPLE	¼ TEASPOON FRESHLY
¼ CUP RED WINE VINEGAR	GROUND PEPPER
¼ CUP HONEY	⅓ CUP DARK RAISINS

1. In a large skillet, heat the olive oil and sauté the onion over medium-low heat until well browned. This will take a while, so don't become impatient.

2. Meanwhile, using a sharp straight-bladed or serrated knife, cut off the leaf crown, skin and eyes of the pineapple. Quarter the pineapple lengthwise and slice out the core; cut the flesh in ½-inch chunks.

Note: The small size of the chunks is important for both cooking down the pineapple juice and for the absorption of the other flavors.

3. When the onion is browned, turn off the heat. Add the vinegar, honey, cinnamon, cayenne, salt and pepper to the skillet. Stir well and simmer over low heat for a minute or two.
4. Add the pineapple chunks and raisins, stir well and cook over medium-high heat for 10 minutes, stirring often. The pineapple will turn a gorgeous reddish brown, the mixture will thicken and the liquid will evaporate.

Let the chutney cool in the skillet, then transfer it to a bowl, making sure to get all the browned bits off the skillet.

Serve as soon as you like, either warm, at room temperature or cool. If you make it ahead, store it in the refrigerator and let the chutney come to room temperature (or close to it) before serving.

This chutney will last at least 4 days in the refrigerator.

Hot and Spicy Raisin

Makes about 1¾ cups This is a chutney you'll want to eat in small amounts, because of its rich, concentrated sweet-hot flavor.

M E N U   S U G G E S T I O N S
Delicious with beef—with burgers, beef pot pie or a savory beef tart, with braised short ribs, with pot roast or sliced brisket. Try it with a pork stew or pork chili, too. For a great vegetarian meal, serve the chutney with Welsh rarebit or with a cheese-sauced noodle pudding, along with a simply cooked green vegetable.

2 FRESH JALAPEÑOS	½ CUP WATER
2 TABLESPOONS MUSTARD OIL (AVAILABLE IN GOURMET SHOPS AND HEALTH FOOD STORES)	½ TEASPOON TURMERIC
	½ TEASPOON PURE GROUND CHILE POWDER
	1 TABLESPOON SUGAR
2 TEASPOONS YELLOW MUS- TARD SEEDS	¼ TEASPOON SALT
¼ CUP FRESH LEMON JUICE	2 CUPS DARK RAISINS (ABOUT 10 OUNCES)

1. Stem, halve, seed and devein the jalapeños; mince. In a medium skillet, heat the oil; when very hot, add the mustard seeds and minced jalapeños and fry for 1 minute. Turn off the heat.
2. Let the mixture in the skillet cool just until you can

Chutney

add the lemon juice and water without spattering and burning yourself. Add the turmeric, chile powder, sugar and salt and bring the mixture to a boil.

3. Stir in the raisins and continue simmering uncovered over low heat for about 20 minutes, until the raisins are very soft and the liquid is almost gone.

4. Puree half the contents of the skillet, then stir the puree back into the raisins in the skillet. Season with a little more salt, if needed.

Let the chutney cool.

Serve warm, at room temperature or cool. Store the chutney in the refrigerator if it's made ahead, and bring it to room temperature (or close to room temperature) before serving.

Covered tightly, the chutney will last at least a week in the refrigerator.

Rich Date Chutney

Makes about 1¾ cups The rich sweetness of dates is the foundation for this spicy concoction that is enhanced by onions, hot pepper and garlic. This chutney is thick and not meant to be eaten in great quantities, but rather as a counterpoint to your main course.

M ENU S UGGESTIONS

Date chutney goes well with roasted lamb, lamb chops or shish kebob. It's also good with a rice-stuffed roasted chicken, a stuffed breast of lamb or a traditional Middle Eastern ground beef dish. A vegetarian meal might consist of couscous made with onions and roasted red pepper and chopped nuts, stuffed zucchini, thick yogurt, hummus and pita.

2 TABLESPOONS NEUTRAL
VEGETABLE OIL (CORN, SAF-
FLOWER, CANOLA OR SUN-
FLOWER)
1 MEDIUM ONION, CHOPPED
1 FRESH JALAPEÑO
2 GARLIC CLOVES, MINCED
½ TEASPOON SWEET PAPRIKA

¼ TEASPOON GROUND CUMIN
½ CUP CIDER VINEGAR
¼ CUP WATER
¼ TEASPOON SALT
1½ CUPS CHOPPED PITTED
DATES (1-PINT CONTAINER
OF WHOLE PITTED DATES)

1. In a medium skillet, heat the oil and sauté the onion until softened.

Meanwhile, stem, halve, seed and devein the jalapeño; mince. Add the minced jalapeño and garlic to the skillet and sauté for another minute or two. Stir in the paprika and cumin and sauté for another minute.

2. Add the vinegar, water and salt to the onion mixture, bring to a simmer and stir over low heat for a minute or two.

3. Stir in the dates and return to a simmer. Continue simmering uncovered over low heat, stirring constantly, for about 2 minutes, until the dates are very soft and the liquid is almost completely gone.

Add more salt if needed and let the chutney cool.

Serve at room temperature or slightly chilled. If made ahead, refrigerate the chutney until about half an hour before needed.

This chutney will last for at least a week in the refrigerator.

Dried-Fig Chutney with

Makes about 2 ½ cups An elegant and sophisticated chutney, with the fragrant overtones of anise, ginger and honey. It will knock the socks off your dinner guests and no one will guess how simple it is to make.

Tip: Calimyrna figs do have naturally thick skins (which helps the pieces of fig maintain their shape during cooking) but you should be careful to buy figs whose thick skins are tender, not rock-hard or leathery.

M E N U   S U G G E S T I O N S
Excellent with roasted duck, chicken or pork. For a meatless meal, try the chutney with a chick-pea or lentil stew, baked eggplant and savory phyllo pastries with cheese filling.

15 DRIED CALIMYRNA FIGS
½ CUP DISTILLED WHITE
  VINEGAR
¼ CUP WATER
¼ CUP HONEY
1 SMALL ONION, CHOPPED
1 TABLESPOON MINCED
  FRESH GINGER
½ CUP BROKEN PECANS(SEE
  NOTE)

¼ TEASPOON ANISE SEEDS
  NOTE: ALTHOUGH FENNEL
  IS OFTEN CALLED ANISE,
  ANISE SEEDS (OR
  ANISEEDS) ARE NOT THE
  SAME AS FENNEL SEEDS.
  BE SURE TO USE ANISE
  SEEDS IN THIS RECIPE.
PINCH OF SALT

Anise Seeds

1. Prepare the figs by snipping or cutting off any hard stem ends and then cutting each fig in eighths.
2. In a medium saucepan, combine all the remaining ingredients (but not the figs) and bring to a simmer, stirring well.

Add the figs and continue simmering uncovered over low heat, stirring often, for about 10 minutes, until the figs are soft. There should be some liquid left in the saucepan because the mixture will absorb more liquid as it cools; if there is no liquid left, stir in ¼ cup water.

Let the chutney cool.

Serve warm, at room temperature or cool. If you've made the chutney ahead, keep it refrigerated until about half an hour before serving.

The chutney will last at least a week if you keep it well covered in the refrigerator.

Note: Don't chop the pecans because the pieces will be too small.

Five-Fruit Chutney

Makes about 2½ cups Dried fruit makes a chutney of rich glistening colors, thick and luxurious in texture, with a tart-sweet flavor. It lasts for several weeks, so it's a good condiment to keep on hand for dressing up your holiday meals.

MENU SUGGESTIONS

Serve this chutney with roasted turkey or chicken, with baked ham or ham steaks, with crown roast of pork, with fine cuts of beef or a flavorful beef daube. For brunch, offer Five-Fruit Chutney to spread on buttermilk biscuits, alongside Canadian bacon or turkey bacon, scrambled eggs and hash brown sweet potatoes. For a vegetarian meal, serve with wild mushrooms in croustades, baked red onions and sautéed escarole.

¼ CUP CHOPPED DRIED PEACHES
¼ CUP CHOPPED DRIED APRICOTS
¼ CUP DRIED PITTED SWEET OR SOUR CHERRIES
¼ CUP DRIED BLUEBERRIES, RAISINS, OR DRIED CURRANTS
2 SLICES DRIED PINEAPPLE, CUT IN SMALL CHUNKS

1 CUP DICED ONION
3 GARLIC CLOVES, MINCED
1 TABLESPOON MINCED FRESH GINGER
¾ CUP RED WINE VINEGAR
¼ CUP WATER
½ CUP SUGAR
½ TEASPOON SALT
¼ TEASPOON HOT RED PEPPER FLAKES

Put all the ingredients in a medium saucepan and bring to a simmer, stirring to dissolve the sugar. Continue simmering uncovered over low heat, stirring often, for about 20 minutes, until all the fruits are soft and the mixture has the consistency of thick jam.

Let the chutney cool.

Serve right away either warm, at room temperature or cool. Store in the refrigerator, well covered, if you plan to hold the chutney for later; take it out about half an hour before serving.

This is long-lasting and will hold up very well for several weeks in the refrigerator, if tightly covered.

Rhubarb-Raisin Chutney

Makes about 2½ cups If you've ever cooked rhubarb, you know that it breaks down into, well... mush, as it cooks. This condiment is more like a thick tangy sauce than a chunky chutney, but it's delicious nonetheless.

MENU SUGGESTIONS

Tart rhubarb complements rich foods such as fried chicken and barbecue, as well as leaner ones—roasted lamb or chicken, sautéed fish (halibut, snapper or turbot, for example), grilled flank steak. For breakfast or brunch, try a savory asparagus tart and chicken or turkey sausage. A tasty vegetarian meal: spoon bread and chutney, with black-eyed peas, sweet potato chips and tender spring greens on the side.

1 POUND RHUBARB
3 TABLESPOONS CIDER VINEGAR
3 TABLESPOONS WATER
⅔ CUP PACKED LIGHT BROWN SUGAR
2 GARLIC CLOVES, MINCED
2 TEASPOONS MINCED FRESH GINGER

1 TEASPOON YELLOW MUSTARD SEEDS
⅛ TEASPOON CAYENNE
PINCH OF CINNAMON
PINCH OF GROUND CLOVES
1 MEDIUM ONION, CHOPPED
⅓ CUP GOLDEN RAISINS

1. Trim the ends of the rhubarb stalks, slit the stalks in half lengthwise and cut in ½-inch slices.

Put the rhubarb and all the remaining ingredients

except the onion and raisins in a medium saucepan and bring to a simmer, stirring to dissolve the sugar. Continue simmering uncovered over low heat for 20 minutes, stirring often.

2. Stir the onion and raisins into the rhubarb mixture and continue simmering uncovered over low heat for 20 more minutes. Watch carefully, stirring often to prevent burning. The mixture should be thick and rough-textured.

Let the chutney cool.

Serve right away at room temperature or refrigerate until slightly chilled. If you make the chutney ahead, refrigerate until about half an hour before serving.

This chutney will last for about a week in the refrigerator.

Spiced Cherry Relish

Makes about 2 cups Make this in June or July when cherries are plump, dark and sweet and you're looking for an interesting new way to eat them.

M E N U   S U G G E S T I O N S
I like this relish with cold chicken or beef, smoked turkey, roasted duck or sliced duck breast—especially on a bed of salad greens dressed with a lemony vinaigrette. For brunch, try the relish on waffles, French toast or a brioche bread pudding, or serve it along with a smorgasbord of smoked fish, herring, tasty cheeses and cucumber salad.

1 ½ POUNDS DARK SWEET CHERRIES	¼ TEASPOON CINNAMON
½ CUP CIDER VINEGAR	¼ TEASPOON GROUND ALL-SPICE
¼ CUP WATER	¼ TEASPOON GROUND CLOVES
¼ CUP SUGAR	PINCH OF SALT

1. Halve the cherries, discarding the stems and pits; reserve.
2. In a medium saucepan, combine the remaining ingredients and bring to a simmer, stirring to dissolve the sugar.
3. Add the cherries and return to a simmer. Continue simmering uncovered over medium heat, stirring of-

ten, for about 20 minutes, until the cherries are tender but not mushy and there is still liquid left in the pan.

Season with a little more salt if needed and let the relish cool.

Serve right away at room temperature or slightly chilled, or refrigerate until about half an hour before needed.

This relish will last about a week in the refrigerator.

Peach or Nectarine Relish

Makes about 2½ cups   Here's a nippy relish to wake up summer appetites. It's simple and refreshing, not too sweet, with a bit of a kick from the scallions and jalapeño. A great way to make the most of summer's best fruit.

MENU SUGGESTIONS

Try this relish with meals you cook or eat outdoors: grilled chicken, beef or lamb; beef or turkey burgers; grilled fish; chicken or duck salad. Good with all kinds of Tex-Mex specialties, too—quesadillas, fajitas, tacos, burritos and tostadas. If you're a vegetarian, serve the relish with grilled vegetables, refried beans and a green salad with avocado.

4 RIPE PEACHES OR NECTARINES (ABOUT **1** POUND)
½ RED BELL PEPPER
2 SMALL OR MEDIUM SCALLIONS
1 FRESH OR BOTTLED JALAPEÑO

1 TABLESPOON EXTRA-VIRGIN OLIVE OIL
1 TABLESPOON FRESH LIME JUICE
1 TABLESPOON SUPERFINE SUGAR
SALT

1. Halve each peach or nectarine by cutting through the flesh along the seam, then gently twisting the halves in opposite directions to separate them. Discard the pits and cut in half again; pare away any hard matter clinging to the centers. Dice the flesh and put the fruit in a large bowl.

2. Devein the red bell pepper and cut in small dice. Trim the scallions and slice thin. Stem, halve, seed and devein the jalapeño; mince. Add the bell pepper, scallions and jalapeño to the large bowl.

3. Add the oil, lime juice, sugar and a pinch of salt to the fruit mixture and stir gently but thoroughly. Allow the mixture to marinate at room temperature for 1 hour, stirring occasionally.

Serve immediately at room temperature or slightly chilled. If you've made the relish ahead, keep it refrigerated until close to serving time.

This relish is at its best on the day it is made, although it's still pretty good on the second day.

Peach Chutney with

Makes about 2 cups This chutney, lightly flavored with brandy and spices, makes wonderful use of ripe, juicy summer peaches. Don't look for excessive sweetness here—it's peachy, not sugary.

MENU SUGGESTIONS

I could just eat this with a spoon, but it's also delicious with summer meals of sliced smoked turkey or grilled chicken, with cold sliced ham or sliced pork roast. For a meatless meal, serve the chutney with a flavorful fish such as bluefish or monkfish or a whole fish grilled outdoors. It's nice at brunch with popovers, herb omelets and crisp bacon.

5 RIPE PEACHES (ABOUT 1½ POUNDS)

2 TABLESPOONS FRESH LEMON JUICE

½ CUP BRANDY

¼ CUP PACKED LIGHT BROWN SUGAR

1 TEASPOON MINCED FRESH GINGER

1 GARLIC CLOVE, MINCED

¼ TEASPOON CINNAMON

⅛ TEASPOON GROUND CLOVES

¼ TEASPOON HOT RED PEPPER FLAKES

2 PINCHES OF SALT

1 SMALL ONION, CHOPPED

1. Peel the peaches: Immerse for 1 minute in a saucepan of simmering water. Remove the peaches from the saucepan and run under cold water until cool enough to handle. The skins will slip off easily.

Brandy

Halve each peach by cutting through the flesh along the seam, then gently twisting the halves in opposite directions to separate them. Discard the pits and cut in half again; pare away any hard matter clinging to the centers. Dice the flesh.

2. Put all the remaining ingredients except the onion and peaches in a medium saucepan and bring to a simmer over low heat, stirring to dissolve the sugar. Continue simmering uncovered over low heat for 5 minutes.

3. Add the peaches and chopped onion and continue simmering uncovered over medium heat for 20 minutes, stirring often, until the peaches are tender and their color has darkened somewhat.

Let the chutney cool.

Serve right away at room temperature or refrigerate until slightly chilled. If you make the chutney ahead, keep it refrigerated until about half an hour before serving.

This chutney will last for at least a week in the refrigerator.

Summer Fruit Chutney

Makes about 2 cups A beautiful amber-and-rosy-red chutney that is tart, a bit spicy and very easy to make. The juicy unpeeled fruit is simply combined with the other ingredients and simmered for half an hour.

MENU SUGGESTIONS

All the obvious summer meals are great with this chutney—grilled chicken or fish, burgers or steak—but try something more unusual: grilled lamb chops or butterflied leg of lamb, grilled kebobs of swordfish and shrimp, an array of pâtés and charcuterie or a savory tart featuring summer vegetables. I love this chutney on sliced summer tomatoes. It perks up rice, polenta and other grains, too.

2 LARGE FIRM-RIPE PEACHES
2 FIRM-RIPE PLUMS
2 FIRM-RIPE NECTARINES
1 TABLESPOON MINCED
  FRESH GINGER
1 GARLIC CLOVE, MINCED
2 TABLESPOONS FRESH LIME
  JUICE
¼ CUP WHITE WINE VINEGAR

¼ CUP ORANGE JUICE
¼ CUP PACKED LIGHT BROWN
  SUGAR
1 TEASPOON YELLOW MUS-
  TARD SEEDS
¼ TEASPOON HOT RED PEP-
  PER FLAKES
SALT

1. Halve each peach, plum and nectarine by cutting through the flesh along the seam, then gently twisting the halves in opposite directions to separate them. Dis-

card the pits and cut in half again; pare away any hard matter clinging to the centers. Dice the flesh.

2. Combine the fruit and all the remaining ingredients including a sprinkling of salt in a medium saucepan and bring to a simmer, stirring to dissolve the sugar. Continue simmering uncovered over low heat for 30 minutes, stirring often toward the end of the simmering time to prevent burning, until the mixture has thickened and the liquid is syrupy.

Let the chutney cool.

Serve right away at room temperature or, if you prefer, slightly chilled. If you make the chutney ahead, refrigerate until about half an hour before needed.

This chutney will last for at least a week in the refrigerator.

Hot Mustard Fruits

Makes about 3 cups This is not precisely a chutney, nor is it a relish, but it's definitely a winner. You'll find it's best served hot or warm.

M E N U S U G G E S T I O N S

There's quite a lot of sauce along with the fruits in this condiment, so it's especially good with simple roasted chicken and turkey, with sliced pot roast and roast beef, with sliced ham, pork or lamb. I like it with wild rice, couscous and all sorts of grains, too.

2 RIPE PEACHES (ABOUT ½ POUND)

3 FIRM-RIPE APRICOTS (½ TO ¾ POUND)

2 RIPE NECTARINES (½ TO ¾ POUND)

2 TABLESPOONS SWEET (UN-SALTED) BUTTER

⅓ CUP PACKED LIGHT BROWN SUGAR

3 TABLESPOONS PREPARED SPICY BROWN MUSTARD

1. Halve each fruit, discard the pit and remove any strings or hard matter from the center. Slice the fruit ¼ inch thick.

2. In a medium saucepan, melt the butter over low heat. Add the sugar and mustard and continue cooking, stirring to dissolve the sugar, for 5 minutes.

3. Gently stir the fruit into the mustard mixture and simmer covered over low heat for 5 minutes, then re-

move the cover and continue simmering for 20 more minutes, stirring occasionally, until the fruit is tender and there is a generous amount of thick sauce in the pan.

Let the fruit cool until it is either hot or warm.

Serve right away, either hot or warm. If you've made the mustard fruits ahead, keep refrigerated until needed and then warm them in a saucepan over low heat.

This condiment will last for at least a week in the refrigerator.

Plum Chutney

Makes about 2 cups Mildly spicy, with real plum flavor. This is a good chutney to make when you don't have much time, since the preparation is quick and the cooking time is short. Be sure to use firm-ripe plums so the chopped fruit will hold its texture during simmering.

M E N U   S U G G E S T I O N S

I like this chutney with smoked turkey or chicken, with chicken paprikash or with any kind of pork. Try it with grilled or roasted duck breast and a puree of autumn root vegetables, too. If you prefer fish, plum chutney is delicious with pan-seared salmon or halibut with a mustard and pepper crust.

1 POUND FIRM-RIPE ITALIAN PRUNE-PLUMS

1 MEDIUM GRANNY SMITH APPLE

1 MEDIUM ONION

1 TABLESPOON NEUTRAL VEGETABLE OIL (CORN, SAFFLOWER, CANOLA OR SUNFLOWER)

½ TABLESPOON MINCED FRESH GINGER

1 GARLIC CLOVE, MINCED

¼ CUP PACKED LIGHT BROWN SUGAR

¼ CUP CIDER VINEGAR

⅛ TEASPOON GROUND ALLSPICE

1 TABLESPOON YELLOW MUSTARD SEEDS

⅛ TEASPOON SALT

1. Cut the plums in half, discard the pits and chop the flesh coarsely, either by hand or with bursts of power

in your food processor. Peel, quarter and core the apple, making sure to remove all the seeds and hard matter from the core; dice the flesh. Dice the onion. Keep these three ingredients separate from each other.

2. In a medium saucepan, heat the oil and sauté the onion over low heat until lightly browned. Add the ginger, garlic and diced apple and sauté for 2 minutes. Add all the remaining ingredients except the plums, stir well and simmer uncovered for 2 minutes.

3. Stir the plums into the apple mixture, cover and simmer over medium-low heat for 10 minutes. Uncover the pan and continue simmering for 10 more minutes, stirring often to prevent burning. Transfer the chutney to a bowl and allow it to cool; it will thicken as it cools.

Serve at room temperature or slightly chilled. If you make it ahead, refrigerate the chutney until about half an hour before serving.

The chutney will last for at least 5 days.

Vegetable Chutneys and Relishes

Fresh vegetable relishes are as traditionally American as apple pie, and we make a lot of very good ones. A couple of the recipes in this section owe their genesis to those traditional relishes (corn relish and chow-chow, for instance) and a few of the chutneys are definitely indebted to the traditional cuisines of India, China, Mexico and Central America, Italy, Thailand and other countries.

For the most part, though, these recipes reflect a newer trend, championed by innovative American chefs, that features relishes and chutneys made with unusual vegetables or made with common vegetables combined in uncommon ways.

Vegetable chutneys and relishes are usually savory or spicy rather than sweet, but (depending on the vegetable involved) some are tart-sweet. As you might expect, many of the relishes are uncooked (and may even serve as salads in a pinch), while most of the chutneys are cooked.

Here's a tip: Be sure to take advantage of locally grown seasonal vegetables whenever you can; they are likely to be the most delicious produce available.

Old-Fashioned Corn Relish

Makes about 1½ cups Perhaps you've tasted a version of this traditional corn relish—the kind Grandmother must have made every summer using corn from her backyard garden. It's sweet and sour and crunchy, with a nice bite of celery seed and turmeric.

MENU SUGGESTIONS

Have an old-fashioned meal with this old-fashioned relish— crisp oven-baked chicken, potato salad, sliced tomatoes. It's good with baked ham or cold cuts, with grilled sausages, with pork or veal chops. For a meatless meal, pair the relish with an egg roulade that has a zucchini and tomato filling.

3 MEDIUM EARS FRESH
  SWEET CORN, OR 1½ CUPS
  THAWED FROZEN CORN
  KERNELS, PATTED DRY ON
  PAPER TOWELS
¾ CUP FINELY CHOPPED
  WHITE CABBAGE
¼ CUP MINCED CELERY
¼ CUP MINCED GREEN BELL
  PEPPER
¼ CUP MINCED ONION

½ CUP CIDER VINEGAR
½ CUP WATER
3 TABLESPOONS PACKED
  LIGHT OR DARK BROWN
  SUGAR
1 TEASPOON ENGLISH-STYLE
  POWDERED MUSTARD
¾ TEASPOON CELERY SEEDS
½ TEASPOON TURMERIC
½ TEASPOON SALT

1. Break each ear of corn in half. Use a serrated knife to cut the kernels from each piece: Place the piece of

corn flat end down on a cutting board. With a sawing motion, cut off several rows of kernels at a time, working from top to bottom slowly (this prevents the kernels from flying all over the place). Do not cut too deeply; you want only the juicy meat of the kernels, not the tough membranes at the base of the kernels. Put the cut kernels in a medium saucepan.

Note: If you're using frozen corn, put the kernels in a medium saucepan.

2. Add the remaining ingredients to the saucepan and bring to a simmer, stirring to dissolve the sugar. Simmer uncovered for about 30 minutes, until the liquid is almost all evaporated and the vegetables are tender. Let the relish cool.

Serve slightly chilled but not icy. If you've made the relish ahead, refrigerate until shortly before serving.

    This relish will last for 3 or 4 days in the refrigerator.

Southwest Corn Relish

Makes about 4 cups No one will argue if you call this a salsa and serve it with blue corn chips as a snack or appetizer. If you're planning to serve the relish with family dinner, you may want to halve the recipe.

M E N U   S U G G E S T I O N S

Great with pork stew, chicken tacos or tostadas, beef fajitas or with any kind of barbecue. At brunch it's delicious with scrambled eggs or western omelets and spicy ranch-style beans. Seafood lovers will enjoy the relish with sautéed red snapper or halibut, red beans and rice, and a side of mild chiles stuffed with cheese.

3 LARGE, 4 OR 5 MEDIUM OR 6 SMALL EARS OF FRESH SWEET CORN, OR 1 (10-OUNCE) PACKAGE FROZEN CORN KERNELS, THAWED

2 MEDIUM-SIZE RIPE GLOBE TOMATOES (ABOUT 1 POUND OR LESS)

1 OR 2 FRESH OR BOTTLED JALAPEÑOS (TO TASTE)

¼ CUP MINCED RED ONION

1 GARLIC CLOVE, MINCED

2 TABLESPOONS EXTRA-VIRGIN OLIVE OIL

2 TABLESPOONS FRESH LIME JUICE

2 TABLESPOONS MINCED FRESH CORIANDER

½ TEASPOON CUMIN SEEDS

SALT

1. Bring a couple of inches of water to a boil in a large pot. Husk the corn, break each cob in half and cook the corn (fresh or frozen) in the boiling water for 1

minute. Drain the corn and cool it quickly under cold running water. Pat dry with paper towels.

If you're using fresh corn, use a serrated knife to cut the kernels from each piece: Place the piece of corn flat end down on a cutting board. With a sawing motion, cut off several rows of kernels at a time, working from top to bottom slowly (to prevent the kernels from flying all over the place). Do not cut too deeply; you want only the juicy meat of the kernels, not the tough membranes at the base of the kernels.

Put the corn in a large bowl.

2. Stem the tomatoes and cut them in small dice. Add the diced tomatoes to the bowl, along with as much of their juice as you can save.

3. Stem, halve, seed and devein the jalapeños; mince. Add the jalapeño, onion and garlic to the bowl. Add the remaining ingredients, including salt to taste, and stir well.

Cover and let the relish marinate in the refrigerator for 1 hour, stirring occasionally.

Serve the relish chilled or bring it to room temperature before serving.

This relish is best on the first day and good on the second, so make it not too long before you'll need it.

End-of-the-Garden

Makes about 3 cups Lucky you, if you have a garden full of tomatoes, peppers and herbs—but try this sprightly, crisp relish even if your garden grows in the local supermarket.

MENU SUGGESTIONS
Summer meals from burgers to grilled steak will benefit from the addition of this relish. I love it simply piled on slices of good French or Italian bread (with extra bread for mopping up the leftover juice) or on baked potatoes, bulgur wheat or brown rice, with dollops of sour cream. The relish also enhances the flavor of tilefish, cod or bluefish.

3 MEDIUM-SIZE SLIGHTLY UNDERRIPE GLOBE TOMATOES (ABOUT 1 POUND), OR 1 POUND PLUM TOMATOES

2 CELERY STALKS

1 GREEN, RED OR YELLOW BELL PEPPER

1 MEDIUM CARROT

¼ CUP MINCED SWEET ONION (SPANISH, BERMUDA OR VIDALIA)

3 TABLESPOONS MINCED FRESH FLAT-LEAF (ITALIAN) PARSLEY

3 TABLESPOONS CHOPPED FRESH HERBS, SUCH AS OREGANO, CORIANDER, ROSEMARY OR CHIVES

3 TABLESPOONS CIDER VINEGAR

1 TABLESPOON NEUTRAL VEGETABLE OIL (CORN, SAFFLOWER, CANOLA OR SUNFLOWER)

½ TEASPOON SUGAR

SALT AND FRESHLY GROUND PEPPER

Tomato Relish

1. Stem the tomatoes and cut them in small dice. Put the diced tomatoes in a large bowl, along with as much of their juice as you can save.

2. Trim the celery stalks; mince. Stem, halve, seed and devein the bell pepper; grate it on the largest holes of a metal grater. Trim and peel the carrot; grate it on the largest holes of a metal grater. Add the celery, pepper and carrot to the bowl of tomatoes.

3. Add the remaining ingredients, including a good sprinkling of salt and pepper, and stir well. Cover securely and let the relish marinate for 1 hour in the refrigerator, stirring occasionally. Taste and add more salt and pepper if needed.

Serve the relish chilled or bring it to room temperature before serving.

   This relish will last for 2 or 3 days in the refrigerator.

Easy Pick-of-the-Season

Makes about 3 cups Chowchow is a mustard-flavored mixed vegetable relish. For this recipe you'll need about 3½ cups of cut-up, raw vegetables to get about 3 cups of chowchow. Traditional chowchow usually includes cauliflower and cabbage; follow the recipe or use any preferred combination of onions, bell peppers, cauliflower, cabbage, green beans, celery, cucumbers, green tomatoes or carrots. To get cauliflower florets of the proper size, cut large florets off the main stems very close to the florets, then break into smaller florets.

M E N U   S U G G E S T I O N S

Take your chowchow along on a picnic or serve it with any summer meal of cold chicken or turkey, burgers, meat loaf or sliced flank steak. It's a good accompaniment to pork roast, smothered pork chops or ham as well. For lunch, serve it with hearty bread, cheese and cold cuts.

1 CUP SMALL CAULIFLOWER FLORETS

1 CUP CHOPPED WHITE CABBAGE

½ CUP DICED RED BELL PEPPER

½ CUP DICED, *SEEDED,* PEELED REGULAR CUCUMBER OR DICED UNPEELED KIRBY (PICKLING) CUCUMBER

½ CUP DICED ONION

¾ CUP CIDER VINEGAR

2 TABLESPOONS WATER

½ CUP SUGAR

1½ TEASPOONS ENGLISH-STYLE POWDERED MUSTARD

½ TEASPOON TURMERIC

1 TEASPOON CELERY SEEDS

1 TABLESPOON YELLOW MUSTARD SEEDS

SALT AND FRESHLY GROUND PEPPER

Chowchow

1. In a large saucepan, bring 6 cups water to a boil with 6 tablespoons salt. With the heat still high, add the cauliflower, cabbage, bell pepper, cucumber and onion and blanch for 1 minute. Immediately drain the vegetables in a strainer and refresh under cold water. Return the drained vegetables to the saucepan.

2. In a small saucepan heat the vinegar, water and sugar and stir to dissolve the sugar. Turn off the heat and whisk in the mustard, turmeric, celery seeds, mustard seeds and a light sprinkling of salt and pepper.

3. Stir the vinegar mixture into the vegetables and bring to a boil. Reduce the heat and simmer, stirring constantly, for 2 to 3 minutes, until the cauliflower is crisp-tender.

Let the chowchow cool, then add more salt and pepper if needed.

Serve at room temperature or refrigerate until chilled. If you make the chowchow ahead, refrigerate until shortly before serving time.

The chowchow will last for at least a week in the refrigerator.

Spicy-Sweet Red and

Makes about 3 cups Here's a lovely way to use the ripe (red) and unripe (green) crop of tomatoes from your garden or your local farmstand or farmers' market. You can't eat too many tomatoes in summer.

MENU SUGGESTIONS

This rich chutney goes beautifully with grilled chicken, burgers, meat loaf or broiled steak served hot or cold. If you prefer, try the chutney with grilled or broiled swordfish, pan-cooked grouper or orange roughy, along with rice and grilled eggplant or zucchini.

2 MEDIUM-SIZE RED GLOBE
TOMATOES (¾ TO 1 POUND)
2 MEDIUM-SIZE GREEN
GLOBE TOMATOES (¾ TO 1
POUND)
1 MEDIUM ONION, CHOPPED
1 CUP LIGHT OR DARK
RAISINS
1 TABLESPOON MINCED
FRESH GINGER
2 GARLIC CLOVES, MINCED
5 TABLESPOONS PACKED
LIGHT OR DARK BROWN
SUGAR

½ TEASPOON SALT
¼ TEASPOON CINNAMON
¼ TEASPOON GROUND
CLOVES
¼ TEASPOON NUTMEG
GRATED PEEL OF 1 LEMON
2 TABLESPOONS FRESH
LEMON JUICE
¼ CUP WATER
¼ TEASPOON HOT RED PEP-
PER FLAKES (OPTIONAL)

Green Tomato Chutney

1. Stem and dice the tomatoes.

2. Put all the remaining ingredients (but not the tomatoes) in a large skillet and bring to a simmer, stirring to dissolve the sugar.

3. Stir the diced tomatoes into the simmering mixture, cover and continue cooking over very low heat for another 15 minutes.

Remove the cover, raise the heat and simmer over medium heat for 30 more minutes, until the chutney is thick and the liquid is reduced to a small amount of syrup.

Let the chutney cool.

Serve right away at room temperature or refrigerate until chilled. If you make the chutney ahead, keep it refrigerated until about half an hour before serving.

This chutney will last for at least a week in the refrigerator.

Fresh Tomato and Dried-

Makes about 2½ cups This is a beautiful red chutney flecked with bright green hot pepper, with a warmly spicy, complex flavor. It's a favorite of mine.

M E N U   S U G G E S T I O N S

Delicious with roasted chicken or sautéed chicken cutlets, with pork roast or with thinly sliced skirt steak. Pair it with brochettes of chicken or swordfish or shrimp—or all three. For vegetarians: Serve the chutney with lentil salad, green salad, flat bread and a creamy cheese—a mild feta cheese would be perfect.

5 TO 7 MEDIUM GLOBE TOMA-
TOES (2½ POUNDS), OR 2½
POUNDS PLUM TOMATOES

15 SMALL DRIED APRICOT
HALVES

1 OR 2 SMALL FRESH
JALAPEÑOS (TO TASTE)

3 TABLESPOONS NEUTRAL
VEGETABLE OIL (CORN, SAF-
FLOWER, CANOLA OR SUN-
FLOWER)

¼ TEASPOON GROUND CUMIN

¼ TEASPOON FENNEL SEEDS

2 TEASPOONS YELLOW MUS-
TARD SEEDS

1 WHOLE DRIED RED CHILE

2½ TABLESPOONS MINCED
FRESH GINGER

1½ TABLESPOONS MINCED
GARLIC

3 TABLESPOONS SLIVERED
OR SLICED ALMONDS (RAW
OR TOASTED)

3 TABLESPOONS SUGAR

SALT

1. Stem and dice the tomatoes. Quarter the apricots. Stem, halve, seed and devein the jalapeños; mince.

Apricot Chutney

2. In a large skillet, heat the vegetable oil and sauté the cumin, fennel seeds, mustard seeds and whole red chile for 10 seconds. Add the ginger and garlic and sauté for 1 minute.

3. Add the diced tomatoes and cook uncovered over low heat for 15 minutes, stirring often. Remove the whole red chile.

4. Stir in the apricots, jalapeños, almonds, sugar and salt to taste and continue cooking uncovered over low heat for 45 minutes more, stirring often, until thick. Let the chutney cool.

Serve right away at room temperature or refrigerate until slightly chilled. If you make it ahead, keep the chutney in the refrigerator until about half an hour before serving.

This chutney will last for at least a week in the refrigerator.

Fruit and Pepper Relish

Makes about 3½ cups The title of this recipe merely hints at how interesting and *três* contemporary this relish is, with its gorgeous colors and textures and a scattering of whole spices. It's a good one to make for a company dinner or party, because it's prepared ahead of time, marinating in the fridge overnight. You must eat it promptly once the marination is complete, however, because the flavor falls off after that.

MENU SUGGESTIONS

This is such a standout that you can keep the meal quite simple—roasted chicken or Cornish hens, fillet of beef, rack of lamb, roast pork loin. Monkfish, tilefish, halibut or swordfish are good choices, too. Vegetarians can serve the relish with a creamy pasta salad and chilled steamed spinach.

1 LARGE RED BELL PEPPER
1 SMALL YELLOW BELL PEPPER
2 SMALL FRESH CHILES, MILD OR HOT (ACCORDING TO TASTE)
1 SMALL ONION
½ CUP GOLDEN RAISINS
½ CUP DRIED, PITTED SWEET CHERRIES
2 GARLIC CLOVES, MINCED

9 THIN SLICES FRESH GINGER
2 TABLESPOONS EXTRA-VIRGIN OLIVE OIL
¼ CUP RED WINE VINEGAR
1 TABLESPOON WATER
12 WHOLE ALLSPICE BERRIES
2 WHOLE CINNAMON STICKS
SALT AND FRESHLY GROUND PEPPER

à la Mode

1. Prepare the vegetables: Stem, halve, seed and devein the bell peppers and chiles. Cut the bell peppers in ¼-inch dice; julienne the chiles. Dice the onion.

2. In a large bowl, combine the vegetables and all the remaining ingredients including a good sprinkling of salt and pepper. Stir well, taste and add more salt and pepper if needed. Cover the bowl securely and let the mixture marinate in the refrigerator overnight, stirring occasionally. You may leave the whole spices and slices of ginger in the relish or remove them.

Serve chilled or let the relish come to room temperature before serving.

As described in the headnote, this relish should be eaten as soon as the overnight marination is complete. The relish will last into a second day, but it's not wonderful after that.

Note: If you leave the whole allspice, cinnamon sticks and slices of ginger in the completed relish, warn your guests not to bite on them.

Roasted Red Pepper Relish

Makes about 3 cups Fine ingredients and simple preparation are the keys here—fresh herbs, good olive oil and homemade roasted peppers. You may alter the amount and variety of herbs according to your preference. For example, my husband is fond of parsley, so I make this with lots of parsley and only a little basil and oregano.

MENU SUGGESTIONS

Wonderful as part of an antipasto or as a condiment with almost anything Italian—pasta, of course, beef braciola, osso buco, veal piccata, gnocchi, you name it. For a different kind of meal, serve the relish with a selection of cured meats, a bowl of aïoli and crisp vegetables, country bread and wedges of strong cheese. For vegetarians: Offer this relish with baked eggplant or eggplant parmigiana, sautéed broccoli raab or cheese ravioli.

4 LARGE RED BELL PEPPERS
¼ CUP PACKED MINCED
  FRESH BASIL, FLAT-LEAF
  (ITALIAN) PARSLEY AND
  OREGANO (TO TASTE—FOR
  EXAMPLE, 2 TABLESPOONS
  BASIL, 1 TABLESPOON
  PARSLEY AND 1 TABLE-
  SPOON OREGANO)

1 GARLIC CLOVE, MINCED
¼ CUP EXTRA-VIRGIN OLIVE
  OIL
¼ CUP BALSAMIC VINEGAR
SALT AND FRESHLY GROUND
  PEPPER

with Fresh Herbs

1.Roast and peel the red peppers (see page 22, How to Roast a Fresh Pepper). Stem the peppers, slit them open and rinse out the seeds. Pat dry on paper towels, then devein. Cut the flesh in strips ¼ inch wide and 2 inches long.

2. In a large bowl, briskly stir together the remaining ingredients, including a light sprinkling of salt and pepper. Add the roasted pepper pieces and stir again. Taste and add more salt and pepper if needed.

Cover securely and let the mixture marinate in the refrigerator for at least 1 hour, stirring occasionally.

Serve chilled or let the relish come to room temperature. If you make it ahead, keep the relish refrigerated until about half an hour before needed.

This relish will last for about 5 days in the refrigerator.

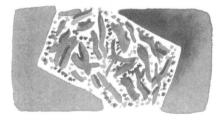

Fennel Relish with

Makes about 4 cups To make this crunchy relish, prepare the vegetables and dressing separately and combine them just before serving. Once they're combined, marinating does no harm; leftovers are still delicious the next day.

The amount here is a little larger than the other recipes; this will allow you to serve the relish as a more substantial side dish if you like.

Tip: I always make this relish with light sour cream, to reduce fat and calories.

M E N U S U G G E S T I O N S

Fennel is delicious with grilled or pan-browned seafood such as salmon, bluefish or squid. If you prefer meat, serve the relish with sliced smoked pork, country ham or veal chops. For brunch, this is great with pickled herring and smoked fish, with bagels or black bread.

2 SMALL FENNEL BULBS
(ABOUT ¾ POUND WITHOUT
STALKS AND LEAVES)
6 RED RADISHES
2 SMALL KIRBY (PICKLING)
CUCUMBERS
¾ CUP REGULAR OR LIGHT
SOUR CREAM

1 TABLESPOON (OR MORE)
FRESH LEMON JUICE
2 TABLESPOONS MINCED
FRESH DILL
SALT AND FRESHLY GROUND
PEPPER

Creamy Dressing

1. Prepare each fennel bulb: Trim the top and stem end close to the globe. Peel off the tough outermost leaf (or two, if necessary). Cut the bulb in half from top to stem, lay each half flat and slice the fennel as thin as possible. Put the pieces in a large bowl.
2. Trim the radishes and slice as thin as possible.

Cut off and discard the ends of the cucumbers; peel partially, to make decorative stripes of alternating green skin and white flesh. Slice the cucumbers as thin as possible.

Add the radish and cucumber slices to the fennel, cover securely and refrigerate until just before serving.
3. In a small bowl, whisk together the remaining ingredients, including a light sprinkling of salt and pepper. Cover and refrigerate until just before serving.
4. Just before serving, add the sour cream mixture to the vegetables and stir well. Taste and add more salt and pepper if needed.

Serve chilled but not icy.

You may prepare and refrigerate the two parts separately a day before needed. Once the fennel and dressing are combined, the relish will last for about 2 days in the refrigerator.

Quick Zucchini Pickles

Makes about 4 cups These aren't pickles in the traditional sense, since they don't require an extended soak in a brine or vinegar solution. In this recipe the zucchini is quickly pickled in a tart, flavorful liquid so it stays crisp and still tastes like zucchini.

MENU SUGGESTIONS

A delicious treat to liven up summer meals of sandwiches, cold chicken and cold sliced meats, cold meat loaf, pasta salad and tomatoes. Good all year round with grilled or pan-cooked bluefish, monkfish, halibut or mahimahi.

4 MEDIUM-SMALL ZUCCHINI (ABOUT 1¼ POUNDS)
1 MEDIUM-SIZE SWEET ONION (SPANISH, BERMUDA OR VIDALIA)
1 CUP CIDER VINEGAR
1 TABLESPOON SUGAR
½ TEASPOON YELLOW MUSTARD SEEDS

1 BAY LEAF
1 TEASPOON CELERY SEEDS
1 TEASPOON TURMERIC
1 TEASPOON ENGLISH-STYLE POWDERED MUSTARD
SALT AND FRESHLY GROUND PEPPER

1. Trim the zucchini and cut each one in half lengthwise. Cut each half in long strips approximately ¼ inch wide; cut the strips down to 1½-inch pieces.

Cut the onion in ½-inch slices and cut the slices into ½-inch pieces.

2. In a large saucepan, combine the remaining ingredients (including a good sprinkling of salt and pepper) and bring to a simmer. Add the onions, stir well and simmer for 3 minutes. Add the zucchini, stir again and cook for 2 more minutes.

Let the mixture cool, stirring occasionally. Add more salt and pepper if needed.

Serve at room temperature or refrigerate until chilled. If you've made the pickles ahead, keep them refrigerated until close to serving time.

These pickles will last for at least a week in the refrigerator.

Cucumber-Parsley Relish

Makes about 3 cups This is a kind of quick pickle that gives you a lot of flavor using few ingredients and minimal effort. Don't try to substitute regular cukes for the Kirbies specified in the ingredients list—it's Kirbies or nothing. Also, it's important to use Japanese rice vinegar (a mild vinegar) so the parsley flavor isn't overwhelmed.

MENU SUGGESTIONS

Offer this refreshing condiment with pork dishes, with stuffed roasted chicken, with sesame-sauced baked chicken or with sesame noodles. Nice with cold sliced beef, too. For brunch, serve the relish with gravlax, smoked salmon or other smoked fish. You can also enjoy cucumber relish with baked fish in black bean sauce and plenty of rice.

6 LARGE KIRBY (PICKLING) CUCUMBERS, EACH ABOUT 5 INCHES LONG (ABOUT 1¾ POUNDS)

SALT

¾ CUP JAPANESE RICE VINEGAR

¼ CUP SUGAR

2 TABLESPOONS CHOPPED FRESH FLAT-LEAF (ITALIAN) PARSLEY

1. Scrub the Kirbies and cut ½ inch off each end. Slice thinly (a mandoline works well for this job) and place the slices in a bowl. Sprinkle the slices generously with salt and mix well with your hands, to be sure all the slices are salted; set aside for 30 minutes.

2. Meanwhile, in a small saucepan, combine the vinegar and sugar and bring to a simmer, stirring to dissolve the sugar. Simmer until the mixture is reduced to ½ cup.

3. Rinse the cucumber slices in a colander and pat dry on paper towels. Transfer the slices to a bowl, add the vinegar mixture and parsley and stir well.

Cover and let the relish marinate in the refrigerator, stirring occasionally, for 1 hour.

Serve chilled or let the relish come to room temperature. If you make it ahead, keep the relish refrigerated until needed.

This relish is at its best on the first or second day, although it will certainly last for 3 or 4 days.

Nippy Cucumber Relish

Makes about 4 cups Nippy, in this case, means the relish has a nice zing but is not mouth-burning. There's plenty of it and it's mild enough to substitute for a salad or vegetable in many meals. It's pretty, too, with the carrot and red pepper lending color to the pale green cukes.

MENU SUGGESTIONS

I like this with stir-fried chicken, sautéed chicken cutlets or marinated baked chicken, with meat loaf or with other simple beef dishes such as steak or hamburgers. It's terrific on sandwiches, too—corned beef or cheese or tuna. This relish complements steamed clams or mussels, a whole baked fish or a savory vegetable tart.

4 LARGE KIRBY (PICKLING) CUCUMBERS, EACH ABOUT 5 INCHES LONG (ABOUT 1¼ POUNDS)

1 MEDIUM CARROT

½ CUP WHITE WINE VINEGAR

2 TEASPOONS MINCED FRESH RED JALAPEÑO (OR OTHER HOT RED PEPPER)

2 TEASPOONS MINCED FRESH GINGER

1 GARLIC CLOVE, MINCED

1 TABLESPOON SUGAR

½ TEASPOON SALT

1. Scrub the Kirbies and cut ½ inch off each end. Cut the cucumbers in large dice and place the diced cucumbers in a bowl.

2. Trim and peel the carrot; grate it on the largest holes of your metal grater. Stir the carrots into the cucumbers.

3. Combine the remaining ingredients in a small saucepan and bring to a simmer; simmer for 2 minutes. Stir the hot vinegar mixture into the cucumbers and let the mixture cool, stirring occasionally. Taste and add more salt if necessary.

Serve right away at room temperature or refrigerate until chilled. If you make it ahead, keep the relish refrigerated until serving time or close to it.

The relish will last for at least 5 days in the refrigerator, but keep in mind that the longer the relish marinates, the hotter it will get.

Spiced Eggplant Chutney

Makes about 2½ cups Eggplant is something of a chameleon in cooking since it turns up in so many dishes in so many cuisines. In this recipe the eggplant has an Indian spin—soft, spicy and a bit sweet, thanks to the currants.

MENU SUGGESTIONS
Delicious with lamb meatballs, leg of lamb or lamb shish kebob, or with simple roasted or baked chicken served with raitas and other Indian dishes. For a meatless meal, try the chutney with broiled swordfish and a mixed grain pilaf.

2 SMALL EGGPLANTS (ABOUT 1 POUND)	¼ TEASPOON TURMERIC
SALT	¼ TEASPOON HOT RED PEPPER FLAKES
¼ CUP EXTRA-VIRGIN OLIVE OIL	2 TABLESPOONS FRESH LEMON JUICE
1 MEDIUM ONION, MINCED	2 TABLESPOONS BALSAMIC VINEGAR
2 GARLIC CLOVES, MINCED	1 CUP WATER
¼ TEASPOON GROUND CUMIN	¼ CUP DRIED CURRANTS
½ TEASPOON POWDERED OREGANO	

1. Trim and peel the eggplants, then cut the flesh in small dice. (The small dice are important for achieving the right texture and flavor.) Put the diced eggplant in a colander, sprinkle generously with salt and toss well to coat. Set aside for 30 minutes.

2. Meanwhile, heat the oil in a large skillet and sauté the minced onion until soft. Add the garlic, cumin,

oregano, turmeric and red pepper flakes and sauté for 1 minute, stirring constantly. Turn off the heat.

3. Rinse the eggplant well and squeeze out the excess liquid one handful at a time. Add the eggplant to the skillet and sauté, stirring constantly, until softened.

4. In a small pitcher, stir together the lemon juice, vinegar and water. Over low heat, gradually pour the liquid into the eggplant mixture, stirring constantly and letting each amount evaporate before adding more. (Adding and evaporating the liquid is an important step in marrying the flavors properly.)

By the time you've used up the liquid, the eggplant should be thoroughly cooked and any browned bits on the skillet should be dissolved and incorporated. If not, add another ¼ cup of water and continue cooking until the liquid is gone.

5. Add the currants and stir for 2 minutes over low heat, until the currants are soft. Season with more salt if necessary and let the chutney cool.

Serve warm, at room temperature or slightly chilled. If you make the chutney ahead, refrigerate until needed or until half an hour before serving.

This chutney will last for 5 or 6 days in the refrigerator.

Sun-dried Tomato Relish

Makes about 3 cups A perfect relish to make in winter, when you long for tomatoes but the garden variety is just a memory. You'll find that the combination of plum and sun-dried tomatoes can be just as satisfying.

M E N U   S U G G E S T I O N S

This relish is particularly good with seafood—with sautéed squid or shrimp, with fillets of red snapper or cod or with a whole baked fish. Serve the seafood with saffron rice or pasta that's been dressed with oil and garlic. If you prefer meat, spoon the relish onto hamburgers or serve with beef fajitas, chicken tacos or tostadas.

5 RIPE PLUM TOMATOES (ABOUT 1 POUND)

5 OUNCES DRAINED, OIL-PACKED SUN-DRIED TOMA-TOES OR 3 OUNCES LOOSE (DRY) SUN-DRIED TOMA-TOES

2 MEDIUM SCALLIONS

3 PICKLED JALAPEÑOS

2 TABLESPOONS COARSELY CHOPPED CORIANDER

2 GARLIC CLOVES, MINCED

1 TEASPOON CUMIN SEEDS

1½ TABLESPOONS FRESH LEMON JUICE

1½ TABLESPOONS EXTRA-VIR-GIN OLIVE OIL

SALT

1. Stem the plum tomatoes and cut them in small dice. If you're using oil-packed sun-dried tomatoes, chop them.

If you are using loose (dry) sun-dried tomatoes, sim-

mer them in a small saucepan of water just until they are soft. Rinse well in cold water, pat dry on paper towels and chop.

Important: Loose sun-dried tomatoes vary in their saltiness. After softening yours as described above, taste one and if it is still very salty, drain the tomatoes and simmer a second time in fresh water for several minutes. Rinse in cold water, pat dry on paper towels and chop.

Put the plum and sun-dried tomatoes in a large bowl.

2. Trim the scallions and slice thinly. Stem, halve and seed the jalapeños; mince. Add the scallions, jalapeños and all the remaining ingredients (including a good sprinkling of salt) to the bowl of tomatoes and stir well. Taste and add more salt and pepper if needed.

Serve immediately or allow the relish to marinate in the refrigerator for an hour, stirring occasionally. Serve chilled or at room temperature. If you've made the relish ahead, keep it refrigerated until needed or until half an hour before serving.

This relish will last for at least a week in the refrigerator.

Punchy Tomatillo-

Makes about 3 cups Tomatillos are often cooked to make green salsas, but they're delicious when used raw, too. They have a bright, tart flavor that works beautifully with mellow plum tomatoes.

MENU SUGGESTIONS
A dollop of this relish will improve almost any Tex-Mex or Santa Fe–style food—stuffed chiles, barbecued beef, burritos, enchiladas and tacos, to name a few. It will liven up burgers (beef or turkey), steak, pork or beef ribs and any simple chicken dish, too. It can be served with red snapper cooked simply, with plenty of beans and rice on the side.

10 TO 15 SMALL OR MEDIUM-
SIZE FRESH TOMATILLOS
(ABOUT ¾ POUND)
4 RIPE PLUM TOMATOES
(ABOUT ½ POUND)
1 SMALL FRESH JALAPEÑO
½ CUP MINCED RED ONION

1 TABLESPOON CHOPPED
FRESH CORIANDER
1 GARLIC CLOVE
2 TABLESPOONS FRESH LIME
JUICE
2 TABLESPOONS TEQUILA
SALT

1. Husk the tomatillos and wash well to remove the sticky substance on the skins. Stem, then chop or dice the tomatillos and place in a large bowl.
2. Stem the tomatoes and cut them in half; scoop out and discard the pulp and seeds. Cut the flesh in small dice and add the diced tomatoes to the bowl,

Tomato Relish

3. Stem, halve, seed and devein the jalapeño; mince. Add the jalapeño, onion and coriander to the tomatillo mixture and stir well.

4. Force the garlic through a garlic press and add the pulp to the bowl, along with the lime juice, tequila and a good sprinkling of salt. Stir well, taste and add more salt if needed. Cover securely and marinate in the refrigerator for 1 hour, stirring occasionally.

Serve chilled or at room temperature. If you make the relish ahead, refrigerate until needed or until half an hour before serving time.

This relish will last for 3 or 4 days in the refrigerator.

Jícama Relish

Makes about 4 cups Crunchy, slightly sweet jícama (pronounced HEE-ka-ma) is ideal for making relish. Look for thin-skinned, smooth specimens free from bruises, withering or cracks. Jícama must be peeled thickly to remove both the brown skin and the tough layer just below the skin.

This recipe makes a lot of relish, so you may want to serve it as a salad or side dish. Remember that it's low in fat, high in fiber and generally terrific—so you can eat as much as you want.

M ENU   S UGGESTIONS

I like this with salmon steaks with a mustard or black pepper coating, with sautéed shrimp or with scallops. It's a refreshing accompaniment to spicy foods such as hot chili, barbecued beef or chicken marinated and baked Moroccan style. For brunch, serve with eggs, Canadian bacon and popovers.

1 JÍCAMA, 4 TO 5 INCHES IN DIAMETER (ABOUT 1¼ POUNDS)

2 MEDIUM NAVEL ORANGES

2 SCALLIONS

1 TABLESPOON SNIPPED FRESH CHIVES

GRATED RIND OF 1 LEMON

2 TABLESPOONS FRESH LIME JUICE

2 TABLESPOONS EXTRA-VIRGIN OLIVE OIL

¼ TEASPOON CAYENNE OR PURE GROUND CHILE POWDER (OR MORE IF YOU LIKE HEAT)

SALT

with Oranges

1. Cut the jícama in half and peel it thickly with a sharp knife, removing the brown skin and the tough layer below the skin. Slice the flesh about ⅛ inch thick; cut the slices in half and then in narrow strips (matchsticks). Put the jícama in a large bowl.

2. Use a sharp straight-bladed knife or a serrated knife to peel the oranges, removing the skin and white pith. Section the oranges, doing the cutting over the bowl of jícama in order to catch the juices; add the orange sections to the bowl.

Trim the scallions and slice the white and green parts as thin as possible; add to the bowl.

3. Add the remaining ingredients (including a good sprinkling of salt) to the jícama mixture and stir well. Cover securely and marinate in the refrigerator for 2 hours, stirring occasionally. Taste and add more salt if needed.

Serve the relish chilled or let it come to room temperature before serving. If you've made it ahead, keep refrigerated until needed or until half an hour before serving.

This relish will last for 5 or 6 days in the refrigerator.

Dilled Beet Relish

Makes about 3 cups Sweet-and-sour beets are enhanced here with fresh dill—a popular combination. I like to top the relish with light or regular sour cream or thick unflavored yogurt.

M E N U   S U G G E S T I O N S

Serve as part of a brunch or party smorgasbord, with herring, kippered salmon, smoked fish. Great with pot roast or corned beef, with country pâté, with cold veal loaf. Instead of coleslaw, serve a heaping spoonful of beet relish with sandwiches—especially with Danish-style open-face sandwiches. For a meatless meal, serve with a potato-mushroom pudding or potato pancakes.

4 MEDIUM-SIZE FRESH BEETS
  (ABOUT 1 POUND WITHOUT
  STEMS AND LEAVES)
½ CUP WHITE WINE VINEGAR
½ CUP WATER
1 TABLESPOON SUGAR

1 TEASPOON DILL SEEDS
¼ TEASPOON SALT
3 TABLESPOONS MINCED
  FRESH DILL
¼ CUP SLIVERED RED ONION
FRESHLY GROUND PEPPER

1. Trim and peel the beets; slice about ⅛ inch thick and then cut in matchsticks or pea-size dice.
2. In a medium saucepan, combine the vinegar, water, sugar, dill seeds and salt and bring to a boil, stirring to dissolve the sugar. Add the beets and stir well. Lower

the heat and cover the saucepan, tilting the lid slightly so steam can escape. Simmer over low heat for 10 minutes, stirring occasionally, until the beets are crisp-tender.

3. Remove the lid from the saucepan and continue simmering over low heat for 10 more minutes, stirring occasionally, until most of the liquid has evaporated.

4. Add the dill, red onion and a light grinding of pepper and stir for a minute or two to blend the flavors and glaze the beets. Let the relish cool, then add more salt if needed.

Serve right away at room temperature or, if you prefer, serve chilled. If you make the relish ahead, refrigerate until about half an hour before needed.

This relish will last for about a week in the refrigerator.

Golden Carrot Chutney

Makes about 3 cups A bowl of this glistening chutney is really pretty with its golden bits of carrot, onion, pepper and pear. It's also quite sweet, so feel free to cut the sugar down to ¼ cup if you like.

MENU SUGGESTIONS

A sweet chutney is especially delicious with salty meats such as ham and smoked pork, but it's equally good with mild-flavored poultry such as turkey or chicken. For a savory brunch, serve alongside cheese blintzes or with cheese omelets. For a vegetarian alternative, prepare couscous laced with zucchini, chick-peas and roasted peppers, and serve the chutney with flat bread and feta cheese.

6 MEDIUM CARROTS (ABOUT 1 POUND)

2 TABLESPOONS NEUTRAL VEGETABLE OIL (CORN, SAFFLOWER, CANOLA OR SUNFLOWER)

1 MEDIUM ONION, DICED

½ YELLOW BELL PEPPER

1 GARLIC CLOVE, MINCED

¼ CUP DICED DRIED PEARS (OR DRIED APRICOTS OR GOLDEN RAISINS)

½ CUP PACKED LIGHT BROWN SUGAR

½ CUP CIDER VINEGAR

½ CUP WATER

½ TEASPOON SALT

PINCH OF GROUND CLOVES

PINCH OF CINNAMON

PINCH OF NUTMEG

PINCH OF GROUND GINGER

PINCH OF GROUND ALLSPICE

¼ TEASPOON HOT RED PEPPER FLAKES

1 TABLESPOON FINELY MINCED SCALLION (GREEN PART ONLY) OR SNIPPED FRESH CHIVES

1. Trim and peel the carrots; mince them or cut them in small dice. Heat the oil in a large skillet, add the carrots and onion and sauté until the onion is translucent.

Meanwhile, cut the bell pepper in small dice.

2. Add the bell pepper, garlic and dried pears to the skillet and sauté just until the pepper softens.

3. Add all the remaining ingredients except the scallions and stir well. Cover the skillet tightly and cook over low heat for 20 minutes, until the carrots are tender but not mushy. Remove the cover and continue cooking, stirring frequently, for 5 more minutes or until the liquid in the skillet evaporates.

4. Turn off the heat, stir in the scallions and let the chutney cool, stirring occasionally. Taste and add more salt if necessary.

Serve at room temperature or slightly chilled. If you make the chutney ahead, keep it refrigerated until about half an hour before needed.

This chutney will last for at least a week in the refrigerator.

Chinese Cabbage Relish with

Makes about 4 cups Sesame dressing would make an old shoe taste good, so you can imagine how delicious this relish is. It's rather like a slaw and, like a slaw, as it marinates the cabbage wilts and softens; after a few hours you'll only have about 3 cups. For maximum crunch, prepare it right before serving.

Tip: The relish is quite tangy at first, but the garlic and ginger calm down fairly quickly.

MENU SUGGESTIONS
Try this relish with stir-fried chicken or pork, with sautéed chicken cutlets or with broiled swordfish steaks. For a very special meal, serve with soft-shell crabs. Vegetarians can have the relish with simple Asian noodle dishes and pan-browned tofu.

1 SMALL CHINESE (NAPA) CABBAGE (½ POUND, ABOUT 4 CUPS SHREDDED AND PACKED)
½ MEDIUM RED BELL PEPPER
½ MEDIUM YELLOW BELL PEPPER
18 SNOW PEA PODS
2 TABLESPOONS PEANUT OIL
1 TABLESPOON TAHINI (SESAME PASTE)

2 TABLESPOONS JAPANESE RICE VINEGAR
1 TABLESPOON SOY SAUCE
1 TABLESPOON HONEY
2 TABLESPOONS WATER
1 GARLIC CLOVE, CHOPPED
1 TABLESPOON MINCED FRESH GINGER
1 TABLESPOON SESAME SEEDS FOR GARNISH

Pepper Confetti and Sesame Dressing

1. Discard any wilted or brown-edged leaves from the head of cabbage and shred enough of the remaining head to make 4 packed cups. Put the shredded cabbage in a large bowl.

2. Stem, seed and devein the bell peppers; cut in small dice. Break off the stem ends of the pea pods; cut the pods in narrow diagonal strips. Toss the peppers and pea pods with the cabbage.

3. In a food processor, blend the remaining ingredients (except the sesame seeds) to make a smooth dressing.

Toast the sesame seeds in a small skillet, stirring over medium heat for 1 or 2 minutes until *golden brown*; be careful not to burn the seeds.

4. Just before serving, add the dressing to the cabbage mixture and toss well. Garnish with toasted sesame seeds.

Serve immediately if you like a really crunchy relish. Alternatively, refrigerate the cabbage relish for an hour or two if you prefer a softer, slightly wilted texture.

This is best eaten on the day you make it, but the relish will last into a second day—limp but tasty.

Tart and Spicy

Makes about 5 cups This is an appealing and colorful relish—and there's a lot of it. The recipe makes enough to call it a salad or side dish, because making less would leave you with a lot of half-used vegetables. Eat the relish as soon as you can because it loses punch after a day or two.

Tip: Keep in mind that the relish must marinate for 2 hours before you eat it, so plan accordingly.

MENU SUGGESTIONS

Crisp-coated oven-baked chicken, hot or cold, goes well with cabbage relish. Take this slawlike relish to your next picnic or backyard meal, to serve with burgers (beef or turkey), cold chicken and sandwiches of all kinds. For vegetarians, make a potato gratin or a frittata with potatoes and farmer cheese, with fried green tomatoes on the side.

1 SMALL WHITE CABBAGE (ABOUT 1 POUND)

1 MEDIUM CARROT

1 SMALL OR ½ MEDIUM RED ONION

1 SMALL YELLOW BELL PEPPER

1 SMALL FRESH OR PICKLED RED JALAPEÑO (OR OTHER HOT RED PEPPER)

2 TABLESPOONS MINCED FRESH FLAT-LEAF (ITALIAN) PARSLEY

2 GARLIC CLOVES

½ CUP WHITE WINE VINEGAR

2 TABLESPOONS EXTRA-VIRGIN OLIVE OIL

1 TABLESPOON WATER

1 TEASPOON YELLOW MUSTARD SEEDS

SALT AND FRESHLY GROUND PEPPER

Cabbage Relish

1. Bring a large saucepan of water to a boil.
Meanwhile, peel any dark green, wilted or blemished outer leaves from the head of cabbage. Quarter the head and cut out the core. Cut each quarter in ½-inch slices and cut the slices down to make ½-inch squares. Trim and peel the carrot; cut it in ⅛-inch slices (coins). *(Note*: Crinkle-cut carrot coins look wonderful in this multicolored, many-shaped relish.)
2. When the water boils, add the carrots and cook for 5 minutes (begin timing from the moment the carrots hit the water); after 5 minutes add the cabbage and cook for 5 more minutes. (The carrots cook for a total of 10 minutes; the cabbage cooks for 5 minutes.)
    Drain immediately in a colander and cool quickly under running water. Shake out excess water. Transfer the vegetables to a large bowl.
3. Slice the onion as thin as possible. Stem, halve, seed and devein both peppers; cut the bell pepper in short, thin slivers and mince the hot pepper. Add the onion, peppers and parsley to the bowl.
4. Force the garlic cloves through a garlic press and put the pulp in a small bowl. Add the remaining ingredients (including a good sprinkling of salt and pepper) and whisk to make a dressing. Pour this dressing over

the cabbage mixture and stir well. Cover the bowl securely and let the relish marinate for 2 hours in the refrigerator, stirring occasionally. Taste and add more salt and pepper if needed.

Serve chilled or at room temperature. If you've made the relish ahead, keep it refrigerated until close to serving time.

Although the relish will last for a couple of days in the refrigerator, it's best to eat it as soon as possible, before it loses character.

Crunchy Cauliflower Relish with Olives and Sun-dried Tomatoes

Makes about 3½ cups   Here's a zingy, crunchy relish with the bright Mediterranean flavors of olives, capers and sun-dried tomatoes.

To get cauliflower florets the proper size, cut larger florets off the main stems very close to the florets, then break the larger florets into florets approximately the size of marbles.

MENU SUGGESTIONS

Turn a simple meal into an interesting one by adding this relish to the menu. Two possibilities: linguine dressed with olive oil and freshly grated Parmesan cheese, a simple green salad and crusty rolls; good sausage or pâté, a flageolet salad dressed with lemon vinaigrette, and toasted French or Italian bread slathered with goat cheese.

⅓ CUP WHITE WINE VINEGAR

3 TABLESPOONS EXTRA-
VIRGIN OLIVE OIL

1 TABLESPOON WATER

1 GARLIC CLOVE, CUT IN
FOUR SLICES

¼ TEASPOON HOT RED PEP-
PER FLAKES

⅛ TEASPOON POWDERED
ROSEMARY

¼ TEASPOON POWDERED
OREGANO

SALT AND FRESHLY GROUND
PEPPER

3 CUPS SMALL CAULIFLOWER
FLORETS (ABOUT ¾ POUND)

10 KALAMATA OLIVES, PITTED

1 TABLESPOON DRAINED
SMALL (NONPAREIL) CA-
PERS

¼ CUP PACKED, DRAINED OIL-
PACKED SUN-DRIED TOMA-
TOES OR LOOSE (DRY)
SUN-DRIED TOMATOES

1. In a small jar, make a dressing by combining the vinegar, oil, water, garlic, hot pepper flakes, rosemary, oregano, a good shake of salt and a few grindings of fresh pepper. Shake vigorously and set aside to allow the flavor to develop.

2. Bring a large saucepan of water to a boil, add the cauliflower and blanch for 3 minutes. Drain in a colander and cool under running water; shake out excess water. Transfer the cauliflower to a large bowl.

3. Chop the olives and add them to the bowl, along with the capers.

If you are using oil-packed sun-dried tomatoes,

chop them and add them to the bowl.

If you are using loose sun-dried tomatoes, simmer them in a small saucepan of water just until they are soft. Rinse in cold water and pat dry on paper towels. Chop the tomatoes and add them to the bowl.

Important: Loose sun-dried tomatoes vary in their saltiness. After softening yours as described above, taste one and if it is still very salty, drain the tomatoes and simmer a second time in fresh water for several minutes. Rinse in cold water and pat dry on paper towels. Chop and add to the bowl.

4. Pour the dressing over the cauliflower mixture and stir well. Cover and allow to marinate in the refrigerator for 1 hour, stirring occasionally. Taste and add more salt and pepper if needed.

Serve chilled or allow to come to room temperature. If you've made the relish ahead, keep it in the refrigerator until needed or until about half an hour before serving.

This relish stays crunchy and delicious for 4 or 5 days in the refrigerator.

Fiery Jalapeño Relish

Makes about 1½ cups Some jalapeños are hotter than others, so your relish may turn out fiery or it may not. Mine has come out both ways using the very same recipe. Keep in mind that when it's hot, this relish really packs a wallop and you'll probably use only small amounts. If you think you'll need more than 1½ cups, double the recipe.

Important: Be sure to wear rubber gloves when working with hot peppers. For more information on hot peppers and working with them, see page 21.

MENU SUGGESTIONS

Garnish sliced steak, pork medallions or sautéed chicken breasts with a dab of crème fraîche and a spoonful of this relish. Use it (cautiously) on sandwiches, tacos or burritos, burgers, steamed or grilled vegetables, scrambled eggs or omelets. If you like seafood, serve as a condiment with seafood stew, on red snapper fillets or on mussels and clams.

6 FRESH JALAPEÑOS
1 RED BELL PEPPER AND 1
  GREEN BELL PEPPER, OR 2
  RED BELL PEPPERS
1 GARLIC CLOVE
½ CUP NEUTRAL VEGETABLE
  OIL (CORN, SAFFLOWER,
  CANOLA OR SUNFLOWER)

2 TABLESPOONS FRESH
  LEMON JUICE
½ TEASPOON SALT

1. Roast the jalapeños and rub off the skins (see How to Roast a Fresh Pepper, page 22). Stem, halve, seed and devein the roasted jalapeños; cut each half in two pieces.

2. Stem, halve, seed and devein the bell peppers; cut them in approximately 1-inch squares.

3. Put all the peppers in your food processor with the remaining ingredients and process in short bursts of power until the pieces are the size of barley. Do not overprocess. Taste and add more salt if necessary.

Serve immediately at room temperature or refrigerate until needed, keeping in mind that the heat from the jalapeños will develop as time goes on. If you make the relish ahead, keep it refrigerated until close to serving time.

This relish lasts for at least 5 days, getting better each day.

Mild Green

Makes about 2½ cups   If you like chiles but can't take heat, this mild chile chutney is for you. It's sweet and soft, with a lovely pepper-apple-tomato flavor and no mouth-burn at all.

This chutney is simply wonderful on sandwiches—cheese, ham, beef, chicken or even grilled vegetables. It makes a terrific dip, too, with tortilla chips or crackers for dunking. I've even served it with my Thanksgiving turkey. For a vegetarian meal, try yellow rice and peas, roasted red peppers and browned leeks, with chutney on the side.

¾ POUND MILD POBLANO CHILES

1 GRANNY SMITH APPLE (6 TO 8 OUNCES)

3 TABLESPOONS NEUTRAL VEGETABLE OIL (CORN, SAFFLOWER, CANOLA OR SUNFLOWER)

1 MEDIUM ONION, DICED

1 MEDIUM GREEN GLOBE TOMATO (ABOUT 6 OUNCES)

2 GARLIC CLOVES, MINCED

2 TEASPOONS MINCED FRESH GINGER

1 TABLESPOON PACKED LIGHT BROWN SUGAR

¼ CUP WHITE WINE VINEGAR

3 TABLESPOONS WATER

SALT

2 TABLESPOONS CHOPPED FRESH CORIANDER

1. Stem, halve, seed and devein the poblanos; dice. Peel, quarter and core the apple, taking care to remove all the seeds and hard matter; dice.

2. Heat the oil in a large skillet, add the chiles, apples

Chile Chutney

and onion and sauté about 8 minutes until the onions are soft.

3. Meanwhile, stem and dice the tomato. Add the tomato, garlic, ginger, sugar, vinegar, water and a good sprinkling of salt to the skillet and stir well. Sauté for several minutes, then cover the skillet and cook over low heat for 5 minutes, stirring several times, until the chutney is thick.

Let the chutney cool, stirring occasionally. Stir in the coriander, then taste and add more salt if necessary.

Serve right away at room temperature or refrigerate until slightly chilled. If you make the chutney ahead, keep it refrigerated until about half an hour before serving.

This chutney is delicious as soon as it's made, but it gets even better after 2 or 3 days. It will last for about 5 days in the refrigerator.

Double Onion–Mango

Makes about 3 cups   Double onions here—small white onions are boiled, a sweet onion is browned and they're both combined with mango and ginger and garlic to make a glorious mélange. This one's a major favorite of mine.

M E N U   S U G G E S T I O N S

Pork chops or an herbed pork roast are very good with this chutney, as are rack of lamb and grilled or roasted chicken. For a vegetarian meal, serve wild rice pancakes and sautéed greens along with the chutney.

12 SMALL WHITE ONIONS (ALSO CALLED BOILING OR PEARL ONIONS), EACH ABOUT 1 INCH IN DIAMETER

1 CUP MANGO OR ORANGE JUICE

1 MEDIUM SWEET ONION (SPANISH, BERMUDA OR VIDALIA)

2 TABLESPOONS SWEET (UNSALTED) BUTTER

1 TEASPOON MINCED FRESH GINGER

1 GARLIC CLOVE, MINCED

SALT

1 ALMOST-RIPE (NOT SOFT) MANGO

1. Peel the small onions: Bring a medium saucepan of water to a boil, turn off the heat and add the onions. Let stand for 1 minute, then drain and run cold water over them. The skins will slip off easily.

2. Return the peeled onions to the empty saucepan, add the fruit juice, cover and bring to a boil. Reduce

Chutney

the heat and simmer covered for 10 minutes, until the onions are tender and the liquid is reduced by half. Cut each onion in half.

3. Meanwhile, cut the sweet onion in ¼-inch slices. In a medium skillet, melt the butter and sauté the sliced onions over medium heat until well browned. Add the ginger, garlic and a light sprinkling of salt and sauté for 2 more minutes.

4. Peel the mango and cut the flesh away from the pit in ¼-inch slices (wherever possible). Cut the slices in bite-size pieces. Add the mango, the halved onions and the reduced liquid to the sliced onions in the skillet. Stir well and simmer uncovered over low heat for 5 minutes. Taste and add more salt if needed.

Let the chutney cool.

Serve right away at room temperature or refrigerate until half an hour before needed. Be sure to let the chutney return to room temperature before serving.

This chutney, kept in the refrigerator, is at its best for about 2 days.

Pickled Onion—Ginger

Makes about 3 cups Spoon this relish onto anything that needs a little perking up. The onions are crisp, though slightly softened by cooking and marinating, and they have the perfume of ginger and a lovely crunch from the mustard seeds.

MENU SUGGESTIONS

Use as a condiment with grilled or pan-cooked chicken cutlets or broiled skirt steak, with vegetable or meat chili or with a savory vegetable tart. Nice as a garnish for a steamed or baked fish such as halibut, cod or bass. Add a dollop of this relish to any plain food—a simple sandwich, scrambled eggs, steamed vegetables—to give it a lift.

1 CUP CIDER VINEGAR	12 THIN SLICES FRESH GINGER
½ CUP WATER	
2 TEASPOONS SUGAR	1 LARGE OR 2 MEDIUM SWEET ONIONS (SPANISH, BERMUDA OR VIDALIA), DICED
½ TEASPOON SALT	
2 TEASPOONS YELLOW MUSTARD SEEDS	
FRESHLY GROUND PEPPER	GRATED RIND OF 1 LEMON

1. In a medium saucepan, combine the vinegar, water, sugar, salt, mustard seeds and a good grinding of pepper. Bring to a boil and stir to dissolve the sugar. Add the ginger, cover the pan and simmer for 10 minutes. Turn off the heat.

Relish

2. Add the diced onion and grated lemon rind to the hot vinegar mixture, stir well and simmer uncovered for 1 minute. Turn off the heat, cover and set aside to let the onions marinate for 1 hour (not in the refrigerator).

Remove the slices of ginger.

Serve right away at room temperature or refrigerate the relish until needed. If you make the relish ahead, keep it refrigerated until about half an hour before serving time.

This relish lasts for at least 5 days in the refrigerator.

Coriander-Yogurt Chutney

Makes about 1½ cups Uncooked chutneys made with fresh herbs and plain yogurt, so familiar at and important to Indian meals, are relatively new to Americans. Use this one and the following recipe as garnishes or condiments or even as sauces. You'll find they are refreshing and cooling, and they add interest to simple foods.

Mincing the coriander by hand preserves the color of the delicate green leaves.

Tip: You may know coriander as cilantro or Chinese parsley, but it's all the same fresh herb.

MENU SUGGESTIONS

Perfect with curries—lamb, chicken, beef or vegetable—or any other highly spiced food. Serve with simple beef, lamb or chicken dishes, with grilled fish or with a vegetarian meal of grain pilaf or rice, Indian-style vegetables and flat bread.

3 TABLESPOONS EXTRA-VIR-
GIN OLIVE OIL

2 TABLESPOONS JAPANESE
RICE VINEGAR

1½ TABLESPOONS FRESH
LIME JUICE

3 TABLESPOONS WATER

1 CUP MINCED FRESH CO-
RIANDER LEAVES (ABOUT 2
CUPS PACKED WHOLE
LEAVES, MINCED BY HAND)

1 TEASPOON MINCED FRESH
JALAPEÑO

3 SHALLOTS, MINCED

½ CUP PLAIN (UNFLAVORED)
YOGURT

SALT AND FRESHLY GROUND
PEPPER

In a medium bowl, whisk together the oil, vinegar, lime juice and water. Stir in the remaining ingredients, including a good sprinkling of salt and pepper. Taste and add more salt and pepper if needed.

Serve immediately at room temperature or refrigerate until needed.

Eat this chutney on the day you make it; it does not last well.

Mint-Yogurt Chutney

Makes about 1½ cups Here's another fresh chutney in the Indian style, similar to the preceding recipe. This one has the clean fresh taste of mint with a nip of ginger.

M E N U   S U G G E S T I O N S
Delicious with lamb in any form—roasted leg, rack, chops or grilled shish kebob. It's also refreshing with tandoori chicken or another nicely spiced baked chicken. Vegetarians may like to serve it with rice pilaf, roasted vegetables and an Indian bread.

GRATED RIND OF 1 LEMON
2 TABLESPOONS NEUTRAL
  VEGETABLE OIL (CORN, SAF-
  FLOWER, CANOLA OR SUN-
  FLOWER)
1½ TABLESPOONS FRESH
  LEMON JUICE
2 TABLESPOONS WATER
½ CUP MINCED FRESH MINT
  LEAVES (ABOUT 1 CUP
  PACKED WHOLE LEAVES)
½ CUP MINCED FRESH FLAT-
  LEAF (ITALIAN) PARSLEY
  (ABOUT 1 CUP PACKED
  WHOLE LEAVES)

1 TEASPOON MINCED FRESH
  JALAPEÑO
1 TABLESPOON MINCED
  FRESH GINGER
1 GARLIC CLOVE, MINCED
½ CUP PLAIN (UNFLAVORED)
  YOGURT
SALT AND FRESHLY GROUND
  PEPPER

In a medium bowl, whisk together the grated lemon rind, oil, lemon juice and water. Stir in the remaining ingredients, including a good sprinkling of salt and pepper. Taste and season with more salt and pepper if needed.

Serve right away at room temperature or refrigerate until needed.

Eat this chutney on the day it's made; it does not last well.